AIR RACING
Over Reno
The World's Fastest Motorsport

PHILIP HANDLEMAN

specialty press
PUBLISHERS AND WHOLESALERS

DEDICATION

To Sonia, my mother, who climbed the fence at Cleveland

and

to Mary, my wife, who cheers her favorite racers at Reno

COPYRIGHT © 2007 BY PHILIP HANDLEMAN

Published by
Specialty Press Publishers and Wholesalers
39966 Grand Avenue
North Branch, MN 55056
United States of America
(800) 895-4585 or (651) 277-1400
www.specialtypress.com

Distributed in the UK and Europe by
Midland Publishing
4 Watling Drive
Hinckley LE10 3EY, England
Tel: 01455 254 450 Fax: 01455 233 737
www.midlandcountiessuperstore.com

ISBN-13 978-1-58007-112-3

Printed in China

Front Cover: *Two Hawker Sea Furies scramble to stay ahead in an Unlimited heat. The backdrop of clear sky and rugged ridgeline is vintage Reno. By the time the Unlimiteds start racing, the temperature has usually peaked and the air is unsettled. Not infrequently the pilots must deal with naturally occurring turbulence in addition to the demands of the racing itself.*

Upper right: *Michael Brown's race 232 September Fury took home the top honors from the 2006 air races. Brown won the 2006 Unlimited Gold race with an average speed of 481.619 mph, which was the second-fastest ever in the sport's 43 years. September Fury basks in its moment of glory.*

Lower right: *The most common types in the Sport class are Lancairs and Glasairs. These two kit-built aircraft are readily available and they provide their owners with high performance at relatively low cost. When the Sport-class races began at Reno in 1998, the paint schemes on these racers were predictably prosaic, but over time they have slowly begun to mirror the flashiness of their cousins in the other classes. This is a Lancair 360, race 4, Unleashed, owned by Airbus A-320 pilot Scott Germain of Phoenix, Ariz. Germain's Lancair is the only Sport class racer equipped with a four-cylinder engine, the Superior XP-400. The smaller engine reflects industry's interest in using the relatively new Sport class races to develop and improve economically viable products for the general aviation market.*

Title Page: *The Griffon-powered Precious Metal has kept decoration to a minimum, but note the cans, connected by a chain, that serve as caps for each exhaust stack. Now that is improvisation.*

Back Cover, Top Left: *The blinding paint scheme of race 5, Voodoo, as seen in the pit in 2002, which was a better year for the souped-up P-51. With Matt Jackson at the controls, Voodoo sprinted to third place in the Unlimited Gold with an average speed of 435.614 mph.*

Back Cover, Top Right: *This standard mid-wing Cassutt III M is maneuvered into an extremely steep bank as it rounds a pylon. Named Midnight Lightning and emblazoned with race number 54, it belongs to pilot Gary Davis of Sanger, Texas, who placed fifth in the 2006 Formula One Silver race with an average speed of 225.262 mph.*

Back Cover, Bottom: *The Formula One racers are arrayed across the runway three abreast. This is possible since the pavement is 150-feet wide. Engines are running to warm up in the frigid morning air. When the signal is given by race officials, the ground crews will dart to the sidelines, and moments later the starter will flag the pilots to begin. Given their light weight, relative high power, and the cool ambient temperature, they will be aloft soon after starting their takeoff rolls, leaving most of the 7,600-foot runway unused.*

TABLE OF CONTENTS

AIR RACING OVER RENO

FOREWORD

ew authors have provided the aviation public with as many high-quality works as Philip Handleman, and none deliver the same combination of photographic artistry, engaging writing, and authoritative knowledge. In this tour de force, the author not only puts you into the cockpit of a 500 mile-per-hour racer, he gives you an appreciation of the desert setting, so you can inhale the intoxicating combination of high-test avgas, the sweet aroma of sagebrush, and visualize the long hours of aerial dueling that range from still mornings to the heat of the afternoon, when dust devils swirl beneath a scorching sun.

Philip's skills, so evident in this fascinating book, have been honed by his more than 35 years as pilot, author, and photographer. The manner in which he combines high drama and intense realism could not be achieved by someone less qualified. In his many years of Stearman ownership, he has learned the true meaning of "wind in the wires," and he conveys this in his work.

There are many other reasons for the high quality of this work. One important one is the long-held passion that the author has had for air racing, a passion tempered by an unusual sensitivity to the subject matter. Philip's mother, Sonia Handleman, grew up near the Cleveland Municipal Airport, attended the races, and then, during the hectic days of World War II, worked at the airport. She poured stories of the fabled airmen and aircraft into Philip's welcoming ear since early childhood, and he has never departed from his lifelong love of air racing. The author uses this intimate knowledge to compose a thumbnail sketch of those fabled Cleveland air races.

Focusing only on his photography, one can see that he is expert in getting the shots that convey the fury of air racing in the most realistic way. No stale, posed photos here, but rather, the essence of air racing is distilled, photo by photo. Because of his knowledge of the scene – the planes, the pilots, the history–he is able to pick his subjects with laser-like skill, and then, when choosing from thousands of possibilities during the editing process, he further refines his artistry by selecting just the very best. The resulting dramatic portfolio of photos represents a historic slice of modern air racing, a record for future historians to use as a source document.

Philip's photos capture not just the beauty and the power inherent in racing airplanes, as inspiring as these are; they also encapsulate the human elements of that strange, even exotic subject, the air racing culture. He knows just how much human effort is applied by the pilots and crews to the preparation of the million-dollar aircraft, making them ready for what may be only a few moments of glorious speed on the course. These photos alone could tell the story of the epic struggles at the Reno race course, but, even better, they are accompanied by insightful text and captions.

Oddly enough, the reverse is true as well. If there were no photographs, reading the text would put the reader at the pylons, in the pit area, in the cockpits, for Handleman delivers the real sense of down and dirty air racing.

This is a book for the collector who wants a record of an event-filled season at Reno. It is a book for the expert, for it provides, in text and photos, a gilt-edge appreciation of a national phenomenon. It is a book for the true race fan, for once read, it will bring the reader back to the subject matter time and again.

Walter J. Boyne
Retired Director
Smithsonian Institution's National Air and Space Museum

ACKNOWLEDGMENTS

This project would not have taken off, if you will pardon the use of an expression from the aeronautical vernacular, were it not for the hard-charging staff of the Reno Air Racing Association, which labors all year long, out of view, to ensure that race week runs smoothly every September. The names of staff members and an army of volunteers remain regrettably shrouded in the fog of the inevitable scramble that accompanies the event, but these devoted workers cheerfully handle the unglamorous chores that make my repeated excursions to Reno so rewarding. They deserve all the thanks in the world.

In her capacity as director of Event Services, Valerie Enos coordinates media access. Her unwavering attention to detail ensures that still photographers, videographers, and film crews get as close to the action as prudence warrants. Despite the many demands that could easily distract a less organized individual, she manages to stay focused and to answer each inquiry with aplomb.

The businesslike efficiency on display at Reno Stead Airport during race week can be attributed to President and Chief Executive Officer Mike Houghton. He combines a human touch with a no-nonsense approach in order to bring the disparate aspects of air racing together in a harmonious collaboration each year. He is assisted not only by his able staff, but by a board of directors and an executive committee comprised of local business and civic leaders who contribute their time and effort to make the Reno air races a world-class aviation event. The management of Reno Stead Airport succeeds each year in readying the runways, taxiways, ramps, hangars, fuel supplies, and the numerous other accoutrements absolutely essential to making the air races occur in grand style.

A special note of thanks goes to the irrepressible Ron Hawes, Formula One guru extraordinaire. Early on the chilly Saturday morning of race week in 2006, with the desert sun reliably beaming its first blinding rays of the day across a still quiet runway, Ron provided transportation to the Formula One starting point. His kindly and accommodating ways made the experience all the more memorable.

No air racing book can be complete without some reference to Cleveland, and in this case the staff at Cleveland State University's library deserve to be recognized. They plucked several historic images out of the *Cleveland Press* Collection that pertain to the halcyon days of air racing in that community so famous for its links to aviation. Thanks are in order for Lynn Duchez Bycko of the library's Special Collections as well as for Vern Morrison and Joanne Cornelius of the library's Digital Production Unit.

The advice and counsel of longtime friend and mentor Walter J. Boyne are appreciated beyond words. Walt is the consummate aviation historian and it is invariably a pleasure to receive his erudite input. As a pilot with more than 5,000 flying hours in aircraft as diverse as the Piper Cub and the B-52, he speaks with uncommon authority on the subject that is our mutual interest.

The staff at Specialty Press shepherded the materials for this book with seeming effortlessness through the complex publication process. At all times, my editor, Nicholas A. Veronico, provided welcome support. No stranger to aviation, Nick's storehouse of knowledge proved to be invaluable. The president of Specialty Press, Dave Arnold, is a fellow aviation enthusiast whose vision and sensibilities have allowed my work on this project to proceed smoothly. Dave's devotion to the subject matter has made a tangible difference for the better.

Most of all I am grateful to my wife, Mary. Her support knows no bounds. On this project as with others completed over the years, she has patiently waited for me to finish a draft so that I could come out and pet the dogs. We have the habit of looking forward to those times that I am between projects because it means there is the opportunity, weather permitting, for me to open the hangar doors, roll out the Stearman, and then fire up the old trainer with Mary aboard. We sail through the invigorating sky together, savoring those precious moments aloft, in touch with ourselves and each other. No one could have a better navigator in flight or in life.

Philip Handleman

About The Author/Photographer

Philip Handleman has been an active private pilot for more than 36 years, and currently owns and flies two aircraft of military lineage, including an open-cockpit Stearman biplane. He belongs to more than 30 aeronautical organizations. As a tireless advocate of aviation, he successfully fought a landmark legal case that defined the limits of municipal control over airport flight activity. He also fostered regulatory protections for users of the U.S. airspace system. His deep attachment to the world of flight is reflected in the 19 prior aviation-related books he has written or edited.

Handleman's popular photography has been published globally in books and magazines. He has received the special recognition of having two of his photographs featured on U.S. postage stamps. The first was his image of the Thunderbirds air demonstration team on the 1997 commemorative stamp honoring the 50th anniversary of the U.S. Air Force. The second was his image of the Cadet Chapel on the 2004 commemorative stamp honoring the 50th anniversary of the U.S. Air Force Academy. As president of the independent production company Handleman Filmworks, he has produced acclaimed public television documentaries, one of which received an Emmy.

Handleman and his wife, Mary, divide their time between their home in Birmingham, Michigan, and a private airstrip in the nearby countryside.

(photo by Donald Sayles)

INTRODUCTION

Like flight testing and combat flying, air racing is a pursuit for the stout of heart. By their very nature, aerial speed contests demand the utmost in pilot judgment and airmanship skill; a minor miscalculation, the slightest inattention to detail, or an ill-considered control input can turn an exhilarating dash into a vexatious contortion with potentially catastrophic consequences.

Striving to be the first to receive the wildly gesticulated wave of the checkered flag at the home pylon requires the flyer, ensconced in his or her cramped cockpit, to squeeze every last ounce of energy out of his or her machine. Dipping the wings in banks around the course markers to lessen the result-ant g-load and throttling forward in the straightaways, with tachometer and manifold pressure gauges at their redlines, is all about pushing the proverbial envelope, about advancing an aerodynamically shaped shell of aluminum alloy or high-tech composites ever faster through the air.

When the pilots finish the last lap they almost instinctively yank back hard on the control stick to gain altitude, that most precious form of money-in-the-bank for a high-performance airplane that has just been flown to the edge. Altitude is the lifesaver if an engine quits. All the experienced hands at the air races know that and fly their ships accordingly.

Six racing classes provided a full schedule of contests during race week at Reno in 2006. Seen here is a Pitts S-1, after having been rolled out of the hangar in preparation for an early morning competition. The voluminous hangar in the background is used to protect the smallest air racing types.

From every angle, the North American T-6 Texan is a beauty. Its curvaceous lines made it a classic from the day it first rolled out of the factory. Almost from the rebirth of air racing at Reno, there has been a racing class comprised of the World War II advanced trainers. The first T-6 class race at Reno occurred in 1968. Race number 12, Thumper, occupies a parking space in the pit area of the Reno Stead Airport.

A legend in its own time, Lyle Shelton's Rare Bear *is a highly modified Grumman Bearcat. This racer is a past Unlimited Gold champion and one of the world's fastest piston-powered airplanes. In 2005, pilot John Penney flew the racer to an impressive win with an average course speed of 466.298 mph.*

For good measure, they bank steeply one last time on the turn from downwind to base. After landing, they slide the canopy aft and, once parked, climb out onto the wing. Then, you can perceive the adrenaline still pumping through their vitalized bodies, a palpable internal electricity powering them to think and act in accelerated increments of time. They project a raw magnetism.

The weather is hot, so the pilots are quick to remove their helmets. You can see that the pilots' heads are drenched in perspiration. The sweat dripping from the brow is, to be sure, a telltale sign of the desert heat and of the stresses of navigating amid a pack of charged competitors, accompanied by the sheer strain imposed by g-forces from the repeated sharp turns on the oblong course.

The pilots also exude of a sense of accomplishment, for not just anybody can do this kind of flying. Air racing officialdom now insists that rookies attend a summer camp. Here they get acquainted with the nuances of maneuvering around pylons at breakneck speeds and learn the rudiments of skimming over the desert at the equivalent of a mere wingspan or two above the buckskin surface.

It is demanding to keep a harness on the heavy iron in the choppiness of the midday heat and capricious gusts. The turbulence can be fearsome by late afternoon. The sweltering desert floor turns into a blowtorch, throwing thermals back up at the sun, and the low-level winds build into a howling tempest. The old fighters and trainers, their tonnage notwithstanding, fall subject to the vagaries of the unsettled air almost as if they are mere toys made of papier-mâché to be jostled upon nature's whim. While wrestling with the buffeting currents, each pilot must be continuously mindful of the competing racers.

Tolerances between airplanes can rapidly shrink to razor-thin. A blink away or an ill-timed hiccup can spell disaster.

Unwavering alertness—what the experts call situational awareness—is imperative. To survive these myriad hazards, the basics of flying must flow as a given. There is no alternative but for the pilots to know their equipment intimately—to be one with the machines at their command. No margin exists for doubt or uncertainty during the few furious minutes of a race.

Trophies and even prize money await the champions, but strolling through the pits where pilots and their crews labor incessantly in tweaking the racing planes it becomes clear that the motivation is predicated on a foundation far more solid than any material reward. In fact, if one were to insinuate to these participants, clad in their oil-stained coveralls or heavily creased flight suits, that the fleeting glory of the winner's circle or the purse that comes with a first-place finish constitutes the purpose for their doing this, the response would likely incorporate a measure of indignation.

Yes, they want to win, but if it were about winning only, then there are significantly less costly and less daring ways to achieve that end—poker, shuffleboard, and badminton come to mind. If there is a common thread linking the teams that explains their motivation, it can be gleaned right here on the ramp during race week.

Camaraderie

In one of those glaring ironies that would seem to defy explanation, in spite of the intense competition, the overarching sensation one feels in the pits is of camaraderie. In the air, the pilots maneuver ferociously for position, doing anything within the strictures of the rules and within the parameters of everyday common sense to gain the lead over the others in the pack. Here, on the shared ramp of the pits, where the racers are parked in close proximity to one another, usually wingtip to wingtip, a different mindset prevails.

Teams that are unrelenting rivals at race time regularly borrow tools from one another in the pits. At dusk, when work gives way to relaxation, barbeques are fired up and the smell of beef on coals wafting through the air serves as an invitation for the competing team members to disregard the temporary ropes that delineate their workspaces. The stanchions come down. Guitars and portable keyboards are hauled out of the teams' big vans and semi-trailers.

Into the night, sometimes under a brilliant moon that casts a silvery sheen over the stationary aircraft, lively music and genial conversation fill the pits. Though the singing is almost always off key, pilots and crew blare out recognizable tunes while others, friends and family among them, gather for the undying joy of fellowship in clusters of folding chairs set up under the wings of silent monsters not yet ready to go snarling around the pylons.

The Ultimate High

A passion for flying lives within all those who climb into the cockpit of a racer. There is more, however. Augmenting

Boise, Idaho-based pilot Holbrook Maslen steeply banks his Shoestring Formula One racer, race number 44, Judy, as he rounds a pylon during the 2006 Reno air races. He placed sixth in the Gold race with an average speed of 230.987 mph.

The Jet class is limited to the Aero Vodochody L-39 Albatros, a trainer/light attack aircraft developed and produced in what is now the Czech Republic. This all-red model is nicknamed Pip Squeak and was flown to victory by former Rare Bear pilot John Penney in 2006 with an average speed of 470.195 mph, a new record for the class.

Modifications to Tom Aberle's Mong racer include this futuristic-looking four-blade propeller. These innovative blades helped to propel race 62, Phantom, to a first-place finish in the 2006 Biplane class with a blazing 251.958 mph average speed. The biplanes had been the perennial laggards at Reno, but with this win, Aberle raised the class from the bottom of the heap. Now the T-6 class has the distinction of having the slowest winner among Reno's six racing classes.

The SNJ-5 is a Navy version of the World War II-vintage T-6 advanced trainer. As the saying goes, they don't make them like this anymore. The aircraft's wings proudly wear the U.S. military's old-style five-pointed star in blue circle with red dot in the middle. The red stripes on the rudder add to the period motif. This gleaming restoration is as much an antique warbird as air racer.

this underlying impulse is the urge to face the unique challenges associated with air racing.

Disinterested commentators and tepid fans have questioned the wisdom of those who choose to engage in a sport as potentially dangerous as air racing, but for the flyers it is the risk itself that serves as a lure. Were scampering around pylons a mundane affair guaranteed to produce safe outcomes, what would be the point, most of the competition pilots would probably ask in a rhetorical retort. Doing practically anything worthwhile, I can hear the aviators declaiming, involves some risk.

The payoff in the risk/reward calculus is the satisfaction that can only come from churning up the course over the mile-high desert floor. Nowhere else but at the annual air races at Reno, Nev., can you legally open up the throttle all the way at just 50 feet off the deck and experience the sensory thrill as clumps of sagebrush slide below in a dizzying blur through the narrow aperture of the racer's sleekly sculpted windscreen.

It is an incredible rush, the ultimate high, for it comes not artificially, but by immersing oneself in the most primal of natural environments—total suspension in the air—with the vantage point of unrestrained velocity. Every once in a while an old speed record falls at the races, symbolizing an advance in the state of the art and denoting a stretch in the all-too-unforgiving and inelastic perimeter of the aeronautical envelope. When this happens, the pilot and crew feel justifiably exultant for the noteworthy accomplishment it represents.

It is not as consequential as penetrating the sound barrier for the first time, but finessing an airplane to fly a little

The newest racing class at Reno is the Jet class, which held its first official competitive race in 2002. The L-39, which originated in the Eastern Bloc during the Cold War, is a practical jet, relatively simple to fly, and inexpensive to maintain. Not surprisingly, many of the type have entered the U.S. market since the Iron Curtain's collapse. When not racing, the jets are parked in the pit area with other types of heavy iron and it is possible, with readily available pit passes, to get almost close enough to the jets to touch them.

faster than it ever has within the high-subsonic regime means that, in a small way, humankind has been advanced. Funny as it may seem, these mostly ragtag teams, impelled by their call to the sky and coping from time to time with adversities as disparate as blown cylinders and inclement weather, are infused with an unvarnished nobility that speaks to the soul of those who wish to make a mark in life.

Reno Ethos

Ahead of every race, the aircraft are wiped clean by the mechanics and handlers and sometimes even the pilots themselves. When the racers leave the pits for a race, the aircraft are shiny specimens in front of the tens of thousands of fans in the grandstands. For the teams it is a matter of pride to always be in the running, looking good, and pouring it on against their competitors in the air.

Since air racing's rebirth at Reno in 1964, the participants who comprise this unique fraternity have developed a distinctive ethos characterized by a boundless audacity in the air and a demonstrable, if at times rollicking, conviviality on the ground. Modern air racing has evolved into a permanent part of the larger aviation culture even though Reno champions are not national heroes like the record-setting racing pilots of the inter-war years.

The resurrected air races have not spawned cutting-edge technologies or breathtaking advances. By the 1960s, the launch pads at Cape Canaveral had become the instrument for reaching higher, faster, and farther. The public was infatuated with the explorers who rode atop mighty booster rockets spouting fiery plumes. With backgrounds as elite test pilots, the astronauts ventured into the precarious void of the final frontier, pushing the astronomical envelope to previously unimagined corners of the cosmos.

Far removed from the headline-making exploits of the astronauts, the members of the fledgling air racing community in the Nevada desert, like their space-faring brethren, held fast to the inviolable spirit of flight. The Reno air races, initially noted for their inelegant setting, quickly came to personify aviation's grassroots. It was flying at its rip-roaring best—a thrill-a-minute, unpretentious, and accessible to all. Reno succeeded then and continues now to stoke the passion of legions of flyers and aficionados.

A stalwart attendee of the Reno air races from the beginning has been Paul Poberezny, the founder of the Experimental Aircraft Association, which, as the world's largest sport pilot organization, is the chief steward of grassroots aviation. Another Reno regular has been Robert A. "Bob" Hoover, the legendary test pilot and air show performer considered by many to be the best pilot in the world. He is best known at Reno for his exacting flying displays in his Shrike Commander and for launching the Unlimited class races from his recog-

Reno is about speed. Here, two P-51 Mustangs battle for position as they scream around the Unlimited course pylons. In the lead is race 6, Flying Dutchman, *flown by Brian Adams, followed closely by race 9,* Cloud Dancer, *with Jimmy Leeward at the controls. No sound compares to a couple of Rolls-Royce Merlin engines running at full throttle. You won't experience anything like it anywhere but the Reno air races.*

nizable P-51 pace plane. From its inception, Reno has also drawn Clay Lacy, a pilot with nearly 50,000 flight hours recorded in his logbook and who competed in that first Unlimited race in 1964, winning the Gold six years later.

The distinguished careers of Poberezny, Hoover, and Lacy hearken back to the saga of prop-driven taildraggers— the way of old-time flying as exemplified by the airmail pathfinders and the barnstorming stuntmen who embraced the realm of the sky and who excelled in it with their seat-of-the-pants skills. Not surprisingly, these three elder statesmen of aviation jumped onto the Reno playing field shortly after the call went out, competing in Unlimited class races during Reno's early years. Each culminated his association with the Reno air races by serving as grand marshal of the event.

As further evidence of Reno's power to light the aviator's fire, one of the original Mercury astronauts came to the air races as an avid participant following his long tenure with NASA. Donald "Deke" Slayton, who had blasted into space in an Apollo capsule on July 15, 1975, could often be seen on the ramp in his latter years tinkering with his diminutive Formula One racer. The famed astronaut received no perquisites or special attention; he was treated as just "one of the guys," which, of course, was one of the reasons he enjoyed the camaraderie of the Reno air races.

The Kingdom of Adventurers

For more than four decades, the Reno air races have embodied the magic of aviation. Pilots come to dare the sky. Like Olympic track-and-field athletes, they throw their heart, nerve, and sinew into the challenge and, figuratively, never look back.

When the cockpit canopies are sealed, props turn, and wings lift the dynamic racers off the pavement. Each flyer becomes the captain of his ship, the master of his fate for the next several minutes. And, out there along the show line in packed grandstands, though far beyond earshot, supporters, fellow airmen, and good-natured buffs wave and cheer, rooting for their favorites.

Each September, Reno's crystalline sky is transformed into the kingdom of adventurers. The pilots return year after year to have their time on the course, however fleeting, during which they might eke out a win or, perchance, break the old record. But whether their heats result in triumph or defeat, they will be at Reno, occupying their special place in the sky, engaged in earnest competition to push their painstakingly honed aircraft to the limits.

In the cockpit, streaking above the desert floor, the pilots are surely alone in the simple physical sense, and their decisions must be made in split seconds. During the moments of gut-wrenching high-g turns or extreme maneuvering to avoid a contestant's vortices, there is no one else in the cockpit to turn to for advice or comfort. Air racing pilots are models of self-reliance.

Yet, the pilots are never truly alone. The aircraft are equipped with sophisticated telemetry systems that allow ground crews to monitor the cockpit gauges in real-time on a laptop computer. This enables the crews to relay any concerns over a discrete frequency. Alarming trends can be addressed immediately.

Also, when not flying, pilots at Reno are accompanied almost all the time by family and ground crew members, who provide an on-site support network during race week. Bolstering the psychic readiness of the pilots is critical.

Full-Color Sketch

Capturing the magnificence of this endearing slice of aviation and then bottling it for consumption has been my mandate. A true depiction requires that posed images be rejected. On one level this is regrettable because the racing planes, festooned in their one-of-a-kind paint schemes, lend themselves to such treatment. Yet, in this case, the aesthetic must be compromised to preserve authenticity, otherwise the viewer would not see air racing as it actually unfolds in the high desert.

Accordingly, the pictures of modern air racing that I have shot and assembled for this book show the aircraft, their pilots and handlers, as well as the larger scene simply as the camera absorbed them in the span of race weeks spread over several years. At times, the ambient light was a photographer's dream while at other junctures it was marginal. Shooting angles usually worked, but were not uniformly optimal. I kept reminding myself that the objective remained a documentary record, not an idealized portrayal.

The aim has been to provide a full-color sketch of the air races as seen through the prism of someone permitted to visit the stands, the static displays, the hangars, the pits, and, most thankfully, the enchanting and inimitable pylons, which demarcate the sandy ground over which the racers thunder. Hopefully, the resultant photo essay offers an accurate visual rendering of what it is like to be at the air races mixed in with the fans, observing the preparations of the ground crews, and hailing the streamlined airplanes as they zoom around the course.

Perhaps in the years to come, people will leaf through these pages and, with a nostalgic sigh, mutter, "Oh, this is the way it was." If so, I will have succeeded. Of course, there can be no substitute for the real thing. If the opportunity presents itself I highly recommend that anyone with the inclination make a point of attending the air races. They are imposing, stimulating, wondrous, and, yes, heaps of fun.

Races, Rules, and Organization

The Reno air races have built a following that includes a core of diehard fans, some of whom travel great distances to be at the annual event. Enthusiasts come from as far away as Europe and the Orient. Spectator attendance during race week regularly aggregates nearly a quarter-million visitors. News from the event is plastered daily over the front page of the local newspaper and broadcast on local television stations. The international aviation media provide extensive coverage, and video segments sometimes appear on national cable channels.

Racing is divided into six separate classes—Unlimited, Biplane, Formula One, T-6, Sport, and Jet. The Unlimited class has been around since the tentative first steps to reintroduce air racing a generation after its postwar disappearance. This class most closely resembles the classic Thompson Trophy races at Cleveland in the 1940s, which famously sparked the imagination of the public. By and large, the Unlimiteds are World War II-vintage fighters highly modified for the rigors of all-out runs around the pylons, and the champion generally chalks up the highest speed of any aircraft among the various racing classes. Speeds in excess of 500 mph have been clocked for a given lap in the Unlimited class, and the highest average course speed for a champion within the class was nearly 488 mph in 2003.

In recent times, curbs to accessibility have brought into question just how "unlimited" the class is today. After years of letting any piston-powered airplane into the class that proved it was fast enough, a minimum empty weight requirement of 4,500 pounds was imposed and the class was changed to an invitational status. Some observers perceive this as an attempt to bar any radical new design from usurping the position of the reigning racers.

Retired airline pilot and current air show pilot Bud Granley has been bringing his North American Texan, race number 9, Lickety Split, *to the Reno air races for many years. The racer's custom paint scheme, reminiscent of the erotic "nose art" that decorated World War II-era aircraft, graces the pit area in between racing heats.*

It has been asserted that the minimum weight requirement and the invitational nature of the competition are concessions to safety. Yet, it has become a subject of debate as to whether these rules are the most effective way to arrive at the desired end state. Given these regulatory developments, one wonders if there is too much of a disincentive for anyone to even try to cobble together an unlimited racer from scratch nowadays. It would seem that if a brand-new, purpose-built, lightweight unlimited-style racer miraculously appeared on the scene, its first order of business would be contending with the standing rules to gain passage onto the course.

The Biplane class racers are traditionally the slowest, and winning speeds tended to hover around the 200-mph mark as they had for decades. In recent years, however, an upward spike took hold due to design innovations.

The Formula One class has long been noted for its engineering ingenuity. Despite engine displacement limits, speeds have risen steadily over the years. These tiny racers have benefited from the incorporation of advances in materials and structures.

In 1968, the T-6 class was added to the racing lineup. These World War II-era advanced trainers are essentially all alike. As might be expected, the speed range over the last couple of decades in the class' races has remained rather narrow—from about 222 mph to 235 mph for the champions. Without radical performance modifications installed on these classics from the 1940s, they have now been surpassed in speed, as a class, by the champions in every other

class. Nevertheless, the extreme similarity of these types and the sheer noise produced by their beefy old round engines make for consistently dramatic contests.

In order to keep the races fresh and to spur renewed interest in the annual event, in 1998 air race organizers augmented the existing classes with a new category under the Sport class banner. The Sport types are largely high-performance, off-the-shelf kitplanes such as those in the Lancair family. Notably, a whole new design called the Nemesis NXT, which emanated from an entrepreneurial effort, has begun to have a tangible impact on the class.

The most recent addition to the racing classes, in 2000, was the Jet class. This was a natural extension of the Reno air races, as jets were a part of the post-war races at Cleveland, and because a relatively easy-to-fly and somewhat affordable Eastern Bloc jet trainer, the L-39, has become available in the U.S. market in growing quantities since the fall of the Iron Curtain. Like the T-6s, these aircraft are evenly matched and post winning speeds each year that are between 434 mph and 470 mph.

Each class has its designated course marked with pylons, which are wooden poles fitted with drums and/or brightly decorated boards for ease of sight. All the courses have an oblong configuration, with each course making use of the same checkerboard home pylon, which represents the finish line for all races. The home pylon is situated about midway along the event's primary runway, a 7,600-foot strip with a generally east-west alignment. The grandstands are arrayed on the runway's south side, facing the home pylon on the opposite side.

The Unlimited and Jet courses are virtually identical as are the Biplane and Formula One courses. The shortest is the Biplane course, which measures 3.1761 miles, and the longest belongs to the Unlimited class, covering 8.4803 miles. All racing classes, except Biplane and Formula One, have air starts, meaning that when airborne they form-up in a line-abreast formation, led by a pace plane, as they approach the course. When all entries are properly aligned, the starter in the pace plane announces the race is underway.

By contrast, the Biplane and Formula One racers have a ground start, referred to by race officials as a "race horse start," in which the competitors are spread out en masse on one end of the runway and receive a flagman's signal to start. Initial starting positions are assigned based on an aircraft's standing in the qualifying heats held earlier in the week. As the week's races unfold and the slower aircraft are weeded out of the progression, starting positions are adjusted according to the prior day's race times.

Through a series of heats during the first four of five days of formal racing, the various classes structure the order of the competitors so that by the last day, Sunday for most racing classes, three championship levels of racing take place—the bronze, silver, and gold. The Unlimited class is the most attentively watched and its Gold Race is, by tradition, the last activity of the last day, the grand finale to a breathtaking week of speed and adrenaline.

In fact, the Unlimited Gold runs eight laps rather than the norm of six. This draws out the drama of the year's premier air race—the contest among indisputably the fastest planes at Reno—and complicates the strategies of the pilots who now must figure out how to cajole or nurse, as the case may be, their temperamental powerplants for an additional 16-plus miles around the already grueling course.

Pilots can be penalized for cutting inside a pylon. Unless the cut was forced by another aircraft, a two-second deduction is applied to the time of the pilot adjudged to

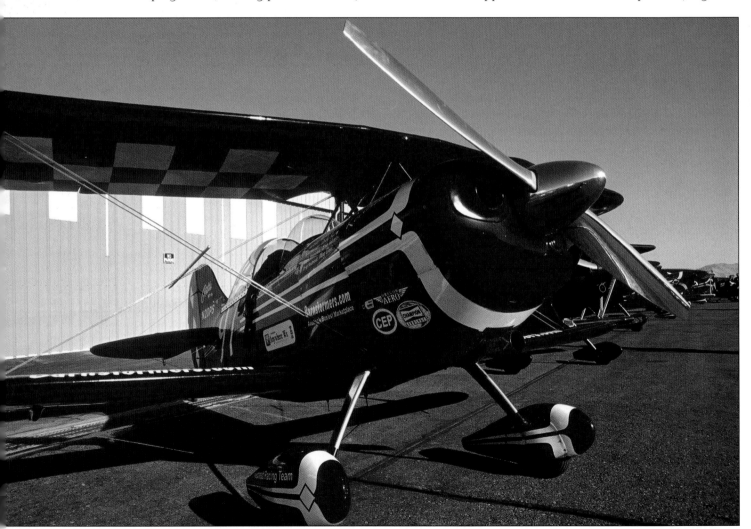

Biplanes line up on the ramp just before their pilots and ground crews get the okay to move them for the start of a contest. The Pitts S-1, an aerobatic staple, is the most prevalent type within the Biplane class.

Appearing to be in coordinated formation, these T-6 class racers are actually jockeying for position as the pilots maneuver over the course. Jim Booth is in front in race number 444, MYT-6, with Wayne Cartwright slightly behind in race 44, Six Shooter. In 2006, both aircraft participated in the Silver contest. Booth finished in third place with an average course speed of 215.296 mph compared to Cartwright's eighth-place 211.709 mph. The combination of the 600-horsepower Pratt & Whitney radial engines and their short propeller blades produces a unique sound that engulfs the desert when the old World War II trainers are fully revved up.

have made the cut. Fortunately, for all concerned, the Reno air races have excellent pylon judges. These individuals faithfully execute their responsibility with an expertise compiled over years of apprenticeship and with a dedication that stems from a deep commitment to their mission in making the event an unreserved success every year. Whether conditions are frigid or boiling, at their remote outposts punctuating the vast expanse of desert that comprises the course the pylon judges can be counted on to accurately and fairly referee the races.

The professionalism demonstrated by the pylon judges far from public view is a critical factor in what makes the air races hum year-after-year. Without the experienced staff and corps of volunteers who have their hearts in the event, there is no way that the air races could occur. So many inconsonant and potentially discordant components must come

together to make the event click—parking, airspace waivers, security, media relations, emergency services, flight operations, concessions, corporate sponsorships, ticket sales, daily sanitation, scheduling, lodging, fueling, and on and on.

Managing the world's fastest motor sport falls in the lap of the Reno Air Racing Association, known as RARA. The organization is overseen by a board of directors made up mostly of local business and civic leaders who understand the beneficial impact of the annual event on the community. Mike Houghton, RARA's president and chief executive officer, brings all the pieces together for what is officially referred to as the Annual National Championship Air Races and Air Show. It is a huge undertaking that almost always runs smoothly thanks to extensive planning and the concerted efforts of the race officials and volunteers working diligently behind the scenes year-round.

CHAPTER ONE

DOMAIN OF DREAMS: CLEVELAND BEGINNINGS AND RENO TRADITIONS

Even before patrons buy their tickets, they are treated to a huge nylon banner setting the tone for the air races. The image of an L-39 jet blends with Reno's pristine sky. Fastened to the flagpoles that are adjacent to the main parking lots, this is the first event-related feature that air race fans are likely to see when they leave their cars for the ticket booth.

As long as there are pilots and airplanes there will be air racing. Indeed, within the decade that Wilbur and Orville Wright first flew their flimsy contraption from the shore at Kill Devil Hill, aviation societies on both sides of the Atlantic organized the first grand aeronautical competitions.

During the week of August 22-29, 1909, a half million spectators gathered for the International Air Meet on the grounds of Bethany Plain, where Joan of Arc's troops once camped, near the town of Reims in the French Champagne region. Elegant grandstands were built adjacent to the airfield that had been cleared for the flying contests. A memorable poster showing a woman attired in bonnet and flowing gown before a procession of aircraft silhouetted against an orange-tinged sky was distributed to promote the air meet.

The airplanes at Reims represented the state of the art. There was Leon Levavasseur's Antoinette, a graceful design resembling the shape of a dragonfly. Other monoplanes included Louis Bleriot's entry based on his famous plane that crossed the English Channel earlier that year and Robert Esnault-Pelterie's R.E.P., a configuration notable

Blurred because of the racer's speed, this historic photograph captures the moment when flying legend Jimmy Doolittle passed the home pylon at the Cleveland Municipal Airport to win the coveted Thompson Trophy in 1932. (Photo courtesy of Cleveland Press Collection, Cleveland State University.)

Flying displays were a big part of the National Air Races. A contingent of these elegant Curtiss P-6E pursuit ships of the 17th Pursuit Squadron from Selfridge Field, near Detroit, participated in the festivities at Cleveland in 1932. (Photo courtesy of Cleveland Press Collection, Cleveland State University.)

The excitement generated by the National Air Races was reflected in the consistently enormous crowds that were drawn to the Cleveland Municipal Airport to see the flying firsthand. This grandstand scene from the 1935 event shows nary an empty seat. Also, the stately observation deck with its catwalks, news media booths, and tower give some idea of the extent to which Cleveland supported the air races. (Photo courtesy of Cleveland Press Collection, Cleveland State University.)

for its expansive tail surfaces. Though the Wright Brothers refused to participate in what they viewed as a frivolous exercise, three of their Wright C models competed. The only American flying in the races was Glenn Curtiss, who brought his comparatively small *Golden Flyer*, a modified version of his original design known as the *June Bug*.

During the week, a variety of contests were held. New records were set for endurance/distance and altitude. Henri Farman, at the controls of one of the enormous airplanes that he and his brother Maurice had built, orbited the course until he nearly froze in the evening sky. He covered 118.5 miles, the longest distance yet tallied in a single

Roscoe Turner, famed air racing pilot of the Golden Age of Flight, was always the showman. Attired in a custom uniform and flying goggles, he flashes his trademark smile for the cameras. He won his third and final Thompson Trophy at Cleveland in 1939 piloting this Laird-Turner Racer. It was powered by a 1,000-horsepower Pratt & Whitney Twin Wasp Sr. engine. (Photo courtesy of Cleveland Press Collection, Cleveland State University.)

flight, in an unprecedented time aloft of more than three hours. Hubert Latham, flying an Antoinette VII, won the altitude competition by climbing to 503 feet above the ground, higher than any of the other pilots.

Each day of the air meet there was a 10-kilometer speed contest called the Tour de Piste. On August 28, the grand finale of these races took place. Sponsored by the wealthy expatriate publisher James Gordon Bennett, it featured a first-place prize of $5,000. For the Bennett race, the course was expanded to two laps of 10 kilometers each. Contestants flew the course separately with their times measured against the clock.

Curtiss opted to fly in severe turbulence, figuring that the unstable air would give him a speed advantage. With no lap or shoulder harness, the bumpiness almost threw Curtiss from his aircraft, but he held on as he later said, "by wedging my feet against the frame." Because he was a champion motorcycle racer (having set the world speed record for motorcycles at 136.3 mph two years earlier), he applied some of his experience rounding turns on race tracks to his flight in the Bennett race. He scored a record time of 15 minutes and 50 seconds, representing an average speed around the course of 47.65 mph.

Reno Stead Airport, located 10 miles northwest of the city, is an inviting place during race week. The main aircraft parking ramp is seen here from the grandstands. In the foreground are exhibitor aircraft. Further back, the Unlimited, T-6, and Jet classes occupy the section of ramp known as the pit. The overhead cloudbank will break in time for the races.

The remoteness of Reno Stead Airport made it a perfect location for air racing when it was selected in the 1960s. The view of the openness from one of the course pylons demonstrates that the site still enjoys substantial isolation, although development has continued on the fringes. During the races, judges position themselves at the base of the pylons to detect any cuts as the racers pass overhead.

Bleriot flew later in the day and it appeared he would win because his first lap was quicker than Curtiss'. But Bleriot's speed dropped in the second lap. When the timekeepers compared their findings, it became apparent that Curtiss had bested Bleriot by a slim 5.4 seconds. Curtiss, who amazingly had a total of only about 10 flying hours, was declared the winner of the Bennett race.

Just six years after humankind's initial powered flight, 38 airplanes came to the Reims air meet. All but two actually flew during the event. Many of these early wood-and-fabric creations suffered an ignominious fate as they and their powerplants were frail and unreliable, but the pilots persisted and throngs of onlookers delighted at the spectacle of so many airplanes taking to the sky. Aviation was a new and exciting endeavor, and the primitive flying machines with trailblazing aviators at the controls represented the first wave of an emerging technology.

For their daring, the pilots were lionized at Reims. Even the disappointment of Bleriot's loss to an American in his native France didn't dampen the spirits of those in attendance. They gave Curtiss a standing ovation. Air racing got a magnificent start at Reims. At the time, an editorial about the air meet in the aviation magazine *Aeroplane* remarked, "Perhaps in only a few years to come the competitions of this week may look pathetically small and the distance and speeds may appear paltry." Those words proved to be prophetic.

On the Way to Cleveland: The Schneider, Pulitzer, and Mitchell Air Races

The James Gordon Bennett races continued each year through 1913. With the successive races, aircraft designs became more streamlined and engines became more powerful. Speeds increased to the point where, by the last pre-World War I Bennett race, the winner, Maurice Prevost, averaged 124.5 mph, more than two-and-a-half times the top speed at the first race four years earlier.

In the same year that Prevost won the Bennett Trophy, he also won the new Schneider race for seaplanes. Underwritten by Jacques Schneider, heir to a French armaments fortune, and held at Monaco on the southern coast of France, Prevost flew a sleek Deperdussin monoplane outfitted with twin floats. The following April, the Schneider race took place again, and this time a diminutive British racing biplane, the Sopwith Tabloid, placed first. Interestingly, the Americans who participated in these pre-World War I races flew European designs, demonstrating that America had fallen behind in aeronautical development.

The war certainly interrupted the sport of air racing, but some of air racing's innovations worked their way into the designs of military pursuit planes. It is noteworthy that Louis Bleriot, who took control of the Deperdussin company and renamed it *Societe Pour Aviation et Derives* (SPAD), employed Deperdussin's talented designer Louis Bechereau. He, in turn, fostered the series of successful combat aircraft renowned for their aerodynamic streamlining. Captain Eddie Rickenbacker, a leading race car driver before the war, became America's ace of aces flying a Bleriot/Bechereau SPAD XIII.

By the war's conclusion, airplanes were performing at a level virtually unimagined when the first air racers galumphed around the course at Reims. With air racing's resumption, the bar had been set very high. Modified military types and scratch-built racers like the incredibly advanced Dayton-Wright RB-1 vied in the 1920 Bennett race held at Estampes in the French countryside. The Dayton-Wright racer incorporated such features as an enclosed cockpit,

Mock pylons flank the main entrance to the viewing areas for the air races. The control tower is in the background.

retractable landing gear, and a single cantilever wing with fore and aft control surfaces. The airplane exceeded 200 mph in flight trials, quite a leap from the pre-war records.

The war's end also brought much of America's aviation industry to the brink. Orders dried up, and the factories that had mushroomed a short time earlier because of war production were facing a reversal of fortunes. Some theorized that staging a major annual air racing event might be an elixir for what ailed the industry. Notably, Ralph, Herbert, and Joseph Pulitzer, Jr., whose family name is indelibly associated with newspaper publishing and journalism's most prestigious award, saw the need for America to regain its preeminence in aviation. They established a new annual speed contest, which first occurred at Long Island, New York's Mitchel Field on Thanksgiving Day in 1920. Army and Navy pursuits competed. An Army Verville-Packard won the Pulitzer Trophy with an average speed of 156.5 mph. In the years that followed, the Pulitzer races were held at Omaha, Nebraska; Selfridge Field north of Detroit; St. Louis, Missouri; Dayton, Ohio; and then back at Mitchel Field.

In 1922, the famed air power advocate Billy Mitchell initiated sponsorship of an annual air race in memory of his late brother John. The new Mitchell race sought to spur the development of military aircraft and to keep U.S. military pilots sharply honed. These races, restricted to the pilots of Selfridge's 1st Pursuit Group, were conducted at the same venue as the Pulitzer races.

Racing champions, often the darlings of the press either because of their ebullient personae or their quiet humility, gained widespread recognition and popularity during this period between the world wars. One example was Navy Lieutenant Alford J. "Al" Williams, a highly regarded pitcher for the New York Giants turned military test pilot. Williams skippered a specially configured Curtiss R2C-1 biplane to victory in the 1923 Pulitzer race at St. Louis with a sizzling speed of 243.67 mph. Another example was Army Lieutenant James H. "Jimmy" Doolittle, a learned test pilot destined for greatness as a World War II air commander. Doolittle flew a variant of the Curtiss R3C-1 to a win at the 1925 Schneider race in Baltimore with an impressive speed for a drag-laden seaplane of 232.573 mph.

In the early 1920s, air racing was perceived as a means of advancing aeronautical technology and improving airplane performance. For an air power advocate like Billy Mitchell, supporting air racing offered the possibility of a meaningful payback to the national defense. With his prodding, select military aircraft were configured expressly for racing, and indeed Army and Navy pursuit planes did very well in the competitions. This was to change, however, as the petulant Mitchell fell out of favor and as development funding for the military air arms failed to keep pace.

The correlation between air racing preeminence and military aviation prowess was perhaps best illustrated by the story of the Schneider race at Lee-on-Solent along the English coastline on September 13, 1931. Reginald J. Mitchell, the ingenious young designer for Britain's Supermarine, conceived the S-6B racing seaplane. It was a masterpiece of sleek lines and graceful curves mounted on twin floats and powered by a 2,300-horsepower, 12-cylinder Rolls-Royce "R" engine.

The pathways to the pylons at the far reaches of the various courses are rugged unpaved lanes that make for bouncy rides. The preferred mode of transportation to these outposts in the open desert are pickup trucks and sport utility vehicles. Invariably, driving out to the pylons causes clouds of dust to kick up and trail behind. If all windows are not sealed shut, fine grains of sand will seep through and leave a thin film over everything inside. This vanity plate is embossed with the acronym "RARA," which stands for Reno Air Racing Association, the official organization overseeing the National Championship Air Races and Air Show.

For lack of budget, the British government refused to fund an entrant in that year's Schneider race. Royal Air Force leaders and aviation enthusiasts were heartbroken. However, Lady Lucy Houston, the widow of a shipping tycoon, offered a reprieve in the form of £100,000 from her personal fortune.

With the necessary funds having been privately donated, in the spring of 1931 preparations were begun for Britain's participation. By autumn everything was ready. Flight Lieutenant J. H. Boothman whipped the S-6B around the course at an average speed of 340.1 mph, a record for either land- or sea-plane. That performance cinched the Schneider Trophy for Britain for the third time.

Later in the month, the S-6B was flown to a speed of more than 400 mph, a record representing the attainment of an important new benchmark. Before the end of the decade, the S-6B racer evolved into the indispensable Spitfire fighter and the "R" engine ripened into the legendary Merlin engine. More than a few informed observers, when asked what several things contributed most to Britain's victory in World War II, point to Lady Houston's magnanimous bestowal to air racing.

Cleveland and the National Air Races

According to air racing historian James P. Wines, the National Air Races began with the second Pulitzer race in 1921 and then leapfrogged from one location to another each year thereafter. The well-known annual Pulitzer race continued through 1925, but ended with the shortsighted cutoff of funding for military racing planes. Nevertheless, air racing continued with major events being held in Philadelphia in 1926, Spokane, Wash., in 1927, and Mines Field (now Los Angeles International Airport) in 1928.

When what some consider the first true National Air Races had their debut in 1929 at the Cleveland Municipal Airport, located on the outskirts of Ohio's largest industrial city, it was no quirk of fate. Fred Crawford, then a vice president of Cleveland-based auto and aircraft valve manufacturer Thompson Products, recognized the value for his city in hosting the air races as well as the public relations benefits to his company by providing sponsorship. Company founder Charles E. Thompson approved the idea, and Crawford handpicked a polished marketing expert, Clifford W. Henderson, to be the event's managing director.

Cleveland's airport was conducive to air racing at the time, as it was one of the largest and most modern facilities of its kind in the world. Farm fields and quaint hamlets, like Berea and Olmsted Falls, surrounded the airport. The city center was a safe 12-miles northeast of the airport. Cleveland was selected as the site of the National Air Races for all but three years during the 1930s.

Crawford and his super-salesman Henderson tirelessly promoted Cleveland's air races. Thanks in part to their efforts, a number of additional companies eventually stepped up as sponsors. Races became identifiable by the sponsors' names, e.g., the Thompson race was the premier pylon contest and the Bendix race was the major cross-country event.

"The National Air Races truthfully may be described as the laboratory of the aeronautical industry," Henderson said at the time. "In them and from them, engineering and aerodynamic problems, safety, comfort, speed, all are advanced." Indeed, some of the civilian racing planes at the time exceeded the speeds of frontline fighters. Backyard mechanics, independent tinkerers, and fledgling factories were originating race-related designs and developing race-related components that might have application to commercial and military aviation.

The aviation industry was still the realm of entrepreneurs rather than industrial giants. Someone with a promising idea and the drive to see it through could build and

The staff and volunteers contribute immensely to making the Reno air races a world-renowned aviation event. Shortly after sun-up, but well before the gates open to the general public, it is not uncommon to spot briefings taking place on the ramp to prepare the personnel for their myriad tasks, mainly accommodating the avid race fans who flock to the grounds in ever-increasing numbers as the week progresses.

fly a hybrid. If it had utility, sales and success might follow. Since aeronautics was still an infant science, no one knew the physical boundaries. The sky was the limit in more than just the figurative sense.

Air-mindedness burgeoned during this era dubbed "The Golden Age of Flight." It was a time of barnstormers and stuntmen entertaining at county fairs throughout Midwestern farm communities. Charles Lindbergh's famous solo trans-Atlantic crossing in the *Spirit of St. Louis* in 1927 captivated countless people, especially the young. The lanky and modest airmail pilot was hailed at parades and banquets.

Flight was seen as an adventurous and dramatic endeavor. A wave of excitement swept the country. Lindbergh became the hero of the century. A whole generation wanted to emulate this instant icon, to follow the flying pied piper into the air.

The National Air Races, scheduled to coincide each year with the long Labor Day weekend, were the venue of choice for aviation enthusiasts. By the time they came to Cleveland in 1929, a half million spectators turned out to enjoy the festivities. Flying displays by some of the greatest pilots of all time, like Doolittle and Williams, were blended into the program. Charles "Speed" Holman even looped a mammoth, all-metal Ford Tri-Motor and then flew it upside down as one of his stunts.

A three-ship Royal Canadian Air Force aerobatic team flying Siskin fighters put on an unusual display that grabbed the crowd's attention. The three planes broke into individual stunt routines and then buzzed the crowd at altitudes low enough that spectators could almost reach up and touch the powerful all-metal biplanes. It was an unforgettable performance, although utterly lacking in safety.

Charles Lindbergh, a mere two years after his historic flight, joined a couple of Navy pilots from Fighting Squadron 1, known as the "High Hats," for daily formation aerobatic performances in the then-new Boeing F4B fighters. The Navy also showed off one of its gargantuan airships, the USS *Los Angeles*, and even had a Vought fighter link up with a trapeze dangling from beneath the dirigible. A sailor climbed down into the open cockpit and the pilot released his aircraft to resume his flight.

Captain Ira Eaker, a rising star among the Army's pilots, flew a Boeing mail plane on a transcontinental mission to prove the concept of being refueled and re-supplied while airborne. On his reciprocal flight, a potentially catastrophic accident ensued. The refueling/re-supply aircraft, a Douglas observation plane, dropped an oil can on the wing of Eaker's plane. Eaker was able to nurse his damaged plane down to the Cleveland Municipal Airport.

A first at the 1929 event was a women's-only cross-country race officially called the Women's Air Derby, but nicknamed the "Powder Puff Derby." On August 18, Clover Field in Santa Monica, Calif., was swarmed by a quarter-million onlookers who came to witness the female pilots take off on their long-distance air race odyssey to Cleveland. Slightly more than half of the 34 women licensed to fly in America at that time were registered to participate in the trailblazing event. Among those flying in the derby were women destined to carve a notch in history—Florence "Pancho" Barnes, Amelia Earhart, Blanche Noyes, Phoebe Fairgrave Omlie, and Evelyn "Bobbi" Trout.

The race was really an endurance run. Routing was not direct but via the lower elevations that hug the Mexican border. Then, at Midland, Texas, the course turned abruptly northward to follow a virtually straight line to Kansas City with a final arc to the finish at Cleveland. The women were to make 16 refueling and rest stops along the way. Plans called for them to overnight at eight of the stops and cover roughly equidistant legs of 350 miles between each. The winner would be the pilot with the shortest flying time.

Tragedy struck early. One of the pilots, Marvel Crosson, spun into the Arizona desert apparently due to the effects of sun exposure at the stop in Yuma. The death cast a pall over the race, but the other contestants kept going. The next day, Claire Fahy's Travel Air biplane was damaged in a forced landing, which removed her from the competition. Pancho Barnes got lost and landed in Mexico. She resumed her flight just in time to avoid detention for her illegal entry. But her airplane was wrecked a day later when she collided with a car upon landing. Margaret Perry came down with typhoid fever in Fort Worth, Texas, necessitating her hospitalization. The Rearwin being piloted by Ruth Nichols hit a tractor when landing at Columbus.

There were assorted other calamities—a groundloop, an in-flight fire, an engine failure—but miraculously 14 of the 20 starters completed the historic race. Louise Thaden, at the controls of a Travel Air, had accumulated the best flying

time—slightly more than 20 hours. The public was enthralled by the novelty of the female pilots racing across a huge swath of the country and the media played to that fascination. The derby represented a milestone in opening up the male-dominated field of aviation to women.

Once at Cleveland, the female pilots who had journeyed so far could compete in a closed-course racing contest for women only on the day after their arrival. Numerous contests for male pilots also took place, some originating on the West Coast and others in Miami, Philadelphia, and Toronto. Contenders like Tex Rankin and Clarence Chamberlain were in the line-ups. Five military races occurred, including the annual Mitchell race.

Unlike the pylon races of the past that required the competitors to fly separately against the clock, most of the closed-course contests at Cleveland entailed the contenders flying the course at the same time. This change heightened the drama of the races. The main racing event was the Labor Day free-for-all that featured five civilian planes and two military aircraft.

To the military's chagrin, a new commercial airplane from Walter Beech's plant in Wichita, Kan., beat the Curtiss Hawk fighters of both the Army and Navy. Douglas Davis smoothly maneuvered his brand-new, shapely red-and-black-trimmed Travel Air "Mystery" to victory with an average speed of 194.90 mph. One of the Hawks came in second at 186.84 mph and the other trailed in fourth place at 153.38 mph.

The standard for air racing in the interwar years was set at Cleveland. The city became synonymous with speed records and aerial derring-do. The flavorful personalities of the flying fraternity, many from barnstorming and military backgrounds, inspired a nation that yearned for heroes during the Great Depression of the 1930s.

The races throughout the 1930s included both pylon and cross-country contests, each with similarly matched aircraft in all shapes, sizes, and colors—among the fastest flying machines of their type. Mixed in with the races were fantastic flying displays by some of the world's finest pilots. In the second half of the Golden Age of Flight, Cleveland became the nerve center of aeronautics, and with a few exceptions hosted the yearly cornucopia of aviation.

In 1931, the Thompson Trophy race, the ultimate in annual closed-close competitions, featured eight air-cooled racers with names like Wedell-Williams, Howard, Altair, Orion, and Gee Bee. Lowell Bayles steered his Gee Bee Super Sportster, a big-barreled creation of the Granville Brothers, to victory at a speed that topped the prior year's race. (In 1930, the first Thompson Trophy race occurred at Chicago, a one-time venue. The race was won by Charles "Speed" Holman at the controls of a hastily built Laird Solution.)

The pylons are course markers for the pilots as they fly at low levels over the desert floor during the air races. This pylon is a simple corrugated drum mounted on a wooden pole. The name and logo of Breitling, the watchmaker and one of the chief sponsors of the air races, appear around the painted metal cylinder.

Scores of vendors display their wares behind the row of bleachers. An amazing variety of merchandise, not all of which is aviation-related, is available in colorful booths that stretch for as far as the eye can see. Art prints, posters, books, sculpted models, program booklets, t-shirts, costume jewelry, ice cream cones, chili dogs, chips, fries, soft pretzels, and, of course, cotton candy are among the staples titillating the tens of thousands of patrons who stroll through concessionaires' alley. The extensive pin collection at this vendor has attracted interest.

The first Bendix Trophy race (sponsored by industrialist Vincent Bendix) started at Burbank, Calif. Jimmy Doolittle flew an improved version of the prior year's Laird Solution, called the Super Solution. He made a couple refueling stops en route to Cleveland and covered the distance in record time. Wishing to set a new transcontinental record, he continued on to Newark where he succeeded in knocking more than an hour off the standing record. Also, in 1931, record-setting pilot Wiley Post and his navigator Harold Gatty brought the globe-girdling *Winnie Mae* to the air races at Cleveland.

Indicative of the pace of aviation advances, the winning Thompson and Bendix speeds were toppled the very next year. A Wedell-Williams piloted by Jimmy Haizlip not only broke the year-old record for the Burbank-to-Cleveland course, but he outdid Jimmy Doolittle's transcontinental record by nearly an hour.

Not to be overshadowed, in 1932, Doolittle flew a new red-and-white Gee Bee R-1, a squat and muscular design that exuded power and speed. He deftly maneuvered the ornery airplane around the pylons in the Thompson race, which, for the first time, consisted entirely of monoplanes. He easily pulled ahead of the field and posted an average speed of 252.686 mph. Earlier Doolittle had throttled the racer's 800-horsepower Pratt & Whitney Wasp Sr. engine all the way forward in Shell Oil's three-kilometer speed dash, exceeding 300 mph and averaging 294.4 mph in the four passes, which represented a new landplane speed record.

With the conclusion of the 1932 National Air Races at Cleveland, Doolittle had collected virtually every major air racing trophy. For someone who obviously thrived on challenges, the air racing world had been conquered. Even more importantly, though, Doolittle, as someone who possessed one of the first doctorates in aeronautics from MIT, could see that air racing was suddenly no longer making major contributions to commercial or military aviation.

More than a decade after the end of World War I, engineers in industry, academia, and government grasped the state of aeronautical science; it was not a paucity of knowledge or even a deficient vision but a lack of funding that hindered progress. Dabbling in a garage on a shoestring budget had rendered major advances, but future breakthroughs would likely necessitate considerable investments in infrastructure, such as large wind tunnels for aerodynamic testing. It would take another world war to jumpstart the process.

Meanwhile, in the 1930s, Doolittle worked in Shell Oil Company's Aviation Division, where he became a leading proponent of 100-octane aviation fuel, an innovation that came in time to enhance the wartime performance of U.S. combat aircraft. When he reactivated his commission in the Army Air Corps shortly before America's entry into World War II, Doolittle soon became one of the many beneficiaries of this improvement.

Civilian racers throughout the remainder of the 1930s were not advancing the state of the art so much as they were entertaining a downtrodden populace otherwise coping with the economic doldrums. The races did not have to be catalysts of scientific invention to be wholly rewarding for the participants and loads of fun for the fans. Before the decade was out, newer military designs started to participate in some of the air

Like the spectators who attended the National Air Races at Cleveland during the Golden Age of Flight, enthusiasts fill the grandstands to see today's National Championship Air Races at Reno.

races, which sharpened the competition and provided a window into what could be expected in the next few years as the country inched closer to war.

In 1934, the National Air Races returned to Cleveland after taking place in Los Angeles the preceding year. The flamboyant Roscoe Turner prevailed in the main races at Cleveland in 1934, winning both the cross-country Bendix and closed-course Thompson Trophies. It was the start of an impressive run for the one-time barnstormer. With later successes in the decade, he became the only pilot to capture the vaunted Thompson Trophy three times.

Roscoe Turner was the archetypal air racing pilot. He appealed to the adventurous instincts in people by presenting himself as the epitome of the swashbuckling aviator. Always appearing in public dressed in his self-designed, military-style uniform, he cut an impressive figure. As part of his self-promotion, he traveled in the company of a pet lion named "Gilmore," the mascot of his oil company sponsor. Sporting a waxed mustache and frequently flashing a toothy grin, Turner was a media favorite.

In the years after the Cleveland air races had concluded, Fredrick Crawford, the Thompson Products executive, liked to talk about how Turner kept afloat financially during the Great Depression. According to Crawford, Turner had "borrowed his wife's savings, mortgaged the home, and put everything he had" into one of Jimmy Wedell's race planes. One day at Cleveland, before a race was to begin, a process server arrived at the airport to repossess the aircraft. A mechanic diverted the man long enough for Turner to fly the race, win, and pay off the debts. "That's how we financed aviation in the 1930s," said Crawford.

Turner was an ardent believer in aviation. Years after he had retired from air racing and adopted the more prosaic lifestyle that came with running an aviation servicing facility in Indianapolis, he advocated the cause of aviation in speeches to audiences who remembered him from his glory days at Cleveland. His outspokenness along with his dashing persona and unparalleled successes on the courses at Cleveland during the Golden Age of Flight inspired many to pursue flying. Another standout personality who made a lasting impression at the Cleveland air races was Claire Chennault. Most famous for his later service as commander of the Flying Tigers in China, Chennault was a crack pilot in his younger years. In 1934, he led a three-ship Army aviation demonstration team that flew formation aerobatics. As a captain, he and his teammates, calling themselves the Men on the Flying Trapeze, flew Boeing P-12s, the last of the Army's biplane fighters, to oohs and aahs from the spectators. It was a performance worthy of an unabashed proponent of air power who during his long and distinguished career clung to the notion of the fighter's primacy.

During the 1930s, Cleveland hosted some of the greatest racing pilots of all time. Benny Howard, developer of the fast cabin monoplane (Howard DGAs, which stood for "Darn Good Airplanes"), designed (with Gordon Israel) the unusual race plane *Mister Mulligan*, the only cabin aircraft among the racers. *Mister Mulligan* surprised many by winning both the Bendix and Thompson Trophies. Harold Neumann, a Kansas farm boy, was always itching to fly racers and teamed up with Howard in 1935 for a stellar year. Steve Wittman, consummate designer of the small racers, believed that weight reduction was a priority, even over power, and that was reflected in his two best-known aircraft, *Chief Oshkosh* and *Bonzo*.

There were more. Jacqueline Cochran, a leading aviatrix who would later establish the Women's Airforce Service Pilots, snared the Bendix Trophy in 1938 flying a modified all-metal Seversky fighter. Tony LeVier, destined to become one of Lockheed's test pilots who flew everything from the P-38 to the U-2, competed in various racers, most notably the Schoenfeldt *Firecracker*.

Frank Hawks, Joe Mackey, Roger Don Rae, Frank Fuller, Milo Burcham, Rudy Kling, Art Chester, Harry Crosby, Paul Mantz, and Earl Ortman were also among the talented pilots who made a mark in aviation history at Cleveland in the prewar years.

Post War Racing at Cleveland

World War II put the races on hold. In 1946, the races were revived in Cleveland, but they were different.

The airplanes in the traditional Thompson race were now piston-powered fighter types that had seen frontline service in the war. It was amazing how much improvement occurred in the relatively short span of time since the last of the pre-war races. In the 1939 Thompson race, Roscoe Turner, piloting his Laird-Turner with a 1,000-horsepower Wasp Sr. engine, racked up an average speed of 282.536 mph. By contrast, in 1946, Alvin "Tex" Johnston won at the controls of a modified Bell P-39Q Airacobra, a World War II fighter type, with a 2,000-horsepower Allison engine that achieved an average speed of 373.908 mph, an improvement over the 1939 winner's speed of more than 32 percent.

To put this 91-mph speed improvement in perspective, when air racing got going again in 1964 after a hiatus of 15 years, Mira Slovak flew a Grumman Bearcat to win what was termed the Unlimited class with an average speed of 376.84 mph, almost identical to the winning speed of 1946. Without the imperative of war, the decade and a half since the first postwar air race saw little meaningful improvement.

It was apparent to many following World War II that piston-powered aircraft had all but reached their performance zenith. Moreover, the revolutionary propulsion technology of the jet engine fostered a modern form of aircraft whose performance vastly eclipsed that of propeller-driven airplanes. People began questioning the point of having closed-course races.

Nevertheless, the postwar air races at Cleveland continued yearly to 1949. That year a tragic crash claimed the life of a pilot as well as that of a mother and her child who were killed when the racing plane veered off course and smashed into their home. The fatalities dampened the usual festive mood at the air races. The incident also highlighted the fact, common to most airports servicing major cities, that sprawl was occurring. Subdivisions began sprouting on farmers' fields. The wide-open spaces around the airport were disappearing.

Compounding the disfavor into which the air races had fallen was the fact that the military would not be able to provide much of a presence at 1950's event because of the Korean crisis. All the factors coalesced to extinguish the air races. Cleveland's fabled annual aviation spectacle, which at times in the postwar period had that same verve evident in the Golden Age of Flight, ceased altogether.

Cleveland Municipal became Hopkins International Airport, and, like all significant hubs in the national airspace system, holding commercial airliners at bay to accommodate air racers rounding pylons would become utterly unthinkable. Accordingly, it was just a matter of time before Cleveland would have to forego the air races in any case.

With the races gone, memories of the fabulous contests, the larger-than-life personalities, and the dazzling air show performances were shared with aviation enthusiasts of the next generation. The spirit of Cleveland lived on in the hearts of adventurers and dreamers. Air racing had not died, but gone into prolonged dormancy.

Air Racing Comes to Reno

History is shaped more often than not by individuals possessing a passion. Circumstances and timing can help. The revival of air racing can be credited to a Nevada pilot and cattle rancher by the name of Bill Stead.

Stead's father had been an Army bomber pilot in World War I, and this quite naturally contributed to his interest in aviation. Another stimulus was the cropdusting at his family's 270,000-acre ranch outside of Reno. Indeed, he was flying by age 16. Moreover, he was drawn to motorsports of all kind from an early age.

Stead had never seen any of the Cleveland air races, but had heard about them firsthand from some pilots who had been there. In the early 1950s, the seed had been planted for the revival of the air races, but Stead started competing in hydroplane races in a serious way and this occupied his otherwise available time. By the end of the decade he had established himself as a national hydroplane champion. Having tackled that challenge, he returned to the idea of jumpstarting the air races.

Coinciding with Stead's returning aviation interest, plans were being developed for the state of Nevada's centennial celebration in 1964. Stead saw this as the opportunity to get air racing going again. With his business and civic connections, he formed a group of local leaders who succeeded in raising the necessary funds from government and private sources to initiate the flying event that he had long contemplated.

The new National Championship Air Races would be an extravaganza entailing not just multiple categories of races, but flying displays that included the Air Force Thunderbirds, national aerobatic and balloon competitions, and skydiving events. The elaborate affair was spread over nine days and the ABC television network provided coverage. Despite extensive planning and Stead's hands-on involvement, Reno's inaugural air races did not occur without glitches.

Everyone agreed that Reno had the undeveloped tracts of land most essential to hosting air races. In addition, Reno was a resort town, accessible by air or highway, with a number of hotels. Accordingly, people who wished to attend would have no problem traveling to Reno and finding accommodations.

The devil proved to be in the details. Exactly where would the races be conducted? Stead surveyed the possibilities and a private airstrip 20 miles east of the city was chosen. Called the Sky Ranch, the property was unfortunately not equipped to handle the volume of air traffic envisioned. The runways were not paved, and every time participants took off and landed clouds of dust billowed, impairing visibility and engulfing the spectators.

Stead had arranged for ABC to televise the racers taking off and landing, but when the potentially hazardous conditions became apparent to the racing pilots they threatened to walk. They wanted to operate from the commercial airport in the city. Tempers flared over Stead's stubbornness and the races almost did not occur.

Partly because of the dust clouds that reduced visibility on takeoff, it was determined that the unlimited racers would not have a "race horse" start as had been the case for racers at Cleveland, but rather these contestants would have an air start. That tradition has held to the present time. Such a start is safer than the alternative, but still carries some risks, especially at the moment the racers break out of the chute and enter the race course. The dangers of six or more aircraft jockeying for position as they enter the race course were manifested when a fatal midair collision occurred during the air start of a T-6 heat in 1994.

The turnout for the inaugural Reno air races was disappointing. Only a few thousand people came to watch the myriad events over the nine days. The site had no control over gawkers who could observe from the roadside or a nearby field. Thus, some people enjoyed the show without having to pay the admission charge.

Despite the difficulties arising from the scarce facilities, the Unlimited class heats elicited much excitement, reminiscent of the fabulous Cleveland events, and provided a glimpse of Reno's promising future. One of the participants in that first championship race was Miroslav "Mira" Slovak who, as an airline pilot in his native Czechoslovakia, had spirited an airplane out of the Eastern Bloc and landed in West Germany where he obtained asylum. He settled in the United States and became a pilot for Continental Airlines.

Because Slovak had an interest in hydroplanes, he befriended Bill Stead, who chose him to fly his Grumman Bearcat in the Unlimited class at the 1964 Reno air races. The scoring methodology at the air races back then was based on the hydroplane point system, which tallied performance of various heats. Under this scoring system, Slovak won first place in the seven-plane field. For those who believe that flight is a metaphor for freedom, Slovak's victory gave the revival of air racing at Reno an auspicious beginning.

The air races remained at the Sky Ranch for only one more year. After that the event was moved to a recently deactivated air base 10 miles northwest of Reno. The base was built in 1942 to train glider pilots. After the war, the Air Force used this remote location in the high desert for survival training. It was also used for helicopter training, and today the Nevada Army National Guard operates CH-47 Chinook helicopters from a separate secure facility on the grounds.

Interestingly, in 1951, the base was named after Bill Stead's brother, Croston, who perished in a flying accident while serving as a fighter pilot with the Nevada Air National Guard. In municipal government hands, the airport became the Reno Stead Airport. This site proved to be considerably better than the prior venue and has continued to serve as the home of the National Championship Air Races and Air Show ever since.

Today there are two main runways, copious ramp space, hangars for the smaller racing planes, fuel storage, a control tower, and perimeter security. Every year, bleachers are erected to seat nearly 40,000 people and a long stretch of asphalt surface is reserved for vendor stalls during race week. Adequate parking areas top off the list of pluses that make this airport ideal for racing teams and the public.

The Reno Stead Airport location is positive in other ways that may not be obvious to the casual attendee. For one thing, the airport's elevation is 5,046 feet. This height of nearly a mile above sea level generally affords the racers better speed than if they were flying at sea level. Also, the next-closest airport of any consequence is Reno Tahoe International Airport, which is sufficiently distant that its air traffic does not meaningfully impact the conduct of the air races. Yet, the bigger airport's accommodation of many major airlines permits easy travel for those wishing to attend the air races from distant locations.

Bill Stead, regrettably, did not live to see the flowering of his dream. In Florida in the spring of 1966, his life ended when the Formula One racer he was flying crashed. At the time of his passing, he had succeeded in building the foundation for the rejuvenation of multi-class national air races, a type of sporting event that is unlike any other in the world. It is a lasting tribute to his vision and perseverance that the air races and the associated air show continue to thrive more than four decades later.

The Reno Races and the Desert Mystique

The motionless air at dawn is filled with the sweet incense-like aroma emitted by the profusion of mesquite that blankets the desert floor. An amber tint bathes the distant mountains that ring this vast flatland. You can look north and see nothing but the sandy terrain, punctuated by sagebrush, the backdrop of the rugged peaks, and the undisturbed sky beyond that fills the rest of the palette. This expansive landscape outside of Reno is still a frontier, wide open and unspoiled.

The day's escalating heat is absorbed by the desert's bed of sand to a point at which the surface begins to bake. In the absence of shade, it actually becomes hot to the touch. As if nature savors playing tricks that confound, the surrounding

The presence of this recognizable group of diehard fans surprises many first-time attendees to the Reno air races. Always attired in orange clothing and seated in Section 3 of the grandstands, these regulars were formed in 1984 when a couple of enthusiasts who did not know each other met at the air races and became fast friends because of their mutual aviation interests. They slowly built a following, which has grown year after year. Now the orange-shirted members of Section 3 represent an unofficial but very reliable support group for the air races, cheering on all the pilots and performers with loud chants and periodic blasts from air horns.

mountains, at their much higher elevations, can actually be snow-capped as one stands perspiring on the sweltering desert floor.

Looking across the course, one will see, every so often, 50-foot high poles with drums affixed on top. These pylons attest to the handiwork of humans in the untamed outback. For a week each September this great basin is transformed into a festival of flying, an empirical manifestation of the species' quest to touch the heavens.

The stillness at daybreak is pierced ever so indelicately when the green flag is waved, signaling the first swarm of racers into the air. The pageant continues with nary an interruption until, by late in the day, the largest, heaviest, loudest machines come blazing around those pylons. The Unlimited aircraft streak past in their flamboyant paint schemes. Skimming on the deck at a respectable fraction of Mach, these fighter planes of a bygone era renew the meaning of flying all-out. It is the ultimate rush for their lucky pilots.

Soon, always too soon, man and machine are spent. Throttles are chopped and landing gear doors opened. Newton's law about things risen having to return is proven again. Slowly, the desert habitat resumes its insular ways, the mountain gods, back to normalcy, can recoup their identity and rest

secure in the knowledge that the day's zealous intruders were of pure heart and noble purpose.

The perfectly proportioned sun, looking more like a placid sphere than a ball of fire, sinks to the ridgeline of the westernmost mountain and hangs there as if balancing on a shelf. It is chilly again and also tranquil. Nature is putting her lid back on the kingdom. Hard as we resist, the day slips irreversibly away. What a great feeling not wanting the day to end!

A vaporous plum-colored luster floods the sky and surrounding mountains. There is equal majesty in the ending as in the beginning. It is a fitting ambiance for the import of the day because the air races represent more than a wholesome titillation of the senses. The air races are an affirmation of the human spirit and the brotherhood of those who fly.

The final remnant of ambient light vanishes behind the far horizon in unhurried retreat with the muted flame of the tired sun. The sky's vibrant blue turns darker and darker until above you it is a sheet of obsidian black, the ideal screen for the tableau of twinkling stars. Perhaps this nighttime show of shimmering suns too distant to ever touch is nature's way to tease the unassuming and earnest souls who try in daylight to conquer the sky. Meanwhile, though, the sound of song and laughter rises from the desert floor. Pilots and crews celebrate their day at the races, anxious for tomorrow when the sky will again be theirs.

CHAPTER TWO

WELCOME RACE FANS: SEE OUR SHOW

The Thunderbirds' trademark diamond formation is seen here. It is a high honor for pilots to be selected for the team. The criteria are demanding and only the best of the best make it aboard. In 2006, Capt. Nicole Mala-chowski, an F-15 fighter pilot with experience enforcing no-fly zones, joined the team. She became the first female pilot to fly with the team.

Everyone likes an air show, and Reno's version is unsurpassed. Dating back to the early days of air racing, organizers recognized the need to keep the ticket-buying attendees occupied and entertained during the inevitable down time between the races. Because Reno has six racing classes with all but the jets flying multiple heats per day, otherwise empty time slots must be filled throughout each of the five days of official racing during race week. The result is an all-day aviation extravaganza alternating between races and flying displays for each of the five official race days.

Little has changed organizationally since the National Air Races of the Golden Age of Flight, when military air demonstration teams, parachutists, solo aerobatic performers, and wingwalkers mesmerized audiences. Spectators crane their necks as one of the expert aerial performers, like Sean D. Tucker, Mike Goulian, Kirby Chambliss, Mike Mangold, or David Martin, shoots into the pure vertical doing violent torque rolls all the way up.

The aerobatic soloists appearing at Reno are so good at what they do that they make their incredible feats look easy. Yes, the modern aerobatic biplanes like the Pitts, customized for air show performances, or monoplanes like the Extra 300 or the CAP 232, offer more capability than the Bucker aerobatic aircraft of the 1930s, but it comes down to what the pilot can do with his airplane. Someone like Sean D. Tucker thoroughly wrings out his tiny biplane in every performance. Sometimes he holds it on the edge of a stall, and other times he rolls inverted and speeds along the show line to clip a ribbon stretched across the runway. All these maneuvers are executed low to the ground where there is absolutely no margin for error.

The late Jimmy Franklin and his partner Eliot Cross often performed at Reno in big old Waco biplanes. They would engage in mock aerial duels, trailing plumes of white smoke as they looped and rolled, leaving a momentary record of their graceful trajectories through the crisp desert sky. In a solo routine, Cross would do an inverted pass in which he held the vertical stabilizer of his hefty biplane so low to the runway pavement that spectators had to avert their eyes for fear that a collision with the ground was imminent. Cross waited until he got to the end of the runway before he rolled positive and pulled up. The sight of his smoke trail arcing upward always caused an audible sigh of relief in the grandstands.

A regular at Reno was the legendary Robert "Bob" Hoover, who excelled at making his flip-flops in the sky

Tucked away on the east ramp are the vast static aircraft displays that, by themselves, would make the Reno air races worth the price of admission. A special section is roped off for one-of-a-kind antiques that have been immaculately restored. These are the beauties competing in the National Aviation Heritage Invitational. Aircraft must be no less than 45 years old and in flyable condition. Sponsored jointly by Rolls-Royce North America, the National Aviation Hall of Fame, the Smithsonian Institution's National Air and Space Museum, and the Reno Air Racing Foundation, the competition culminates with the presentation of the Rolls-Royce Aviation Heritage Trophy to the most authentically restored aircraft.

appear as second nature to him. As a World War II fighter pilot, postwar test pilot, and longtime air show performer, he brought more experience to the show line in the later years of his performing than any other pilot. He knew his airplanes inside and out, a quality he honed after the war as the Air Force's backup pilot to the legendary Chuck Yeager on the first supersonic plane, the Bell X-1.

At Reno, Hoover would put his Shrike Commander, a twin-engine executive transport, through an aerobatic series including aerial reversals, Cuban eights, and, for sheer drama, would shut off both engines and execute perfect point rolls precisely coordinated to be halfway done at the center of the crowd line. Pilots were more amazed than anyone in the audience since they knew that this airplane was built for comfortable cross-country business trips, not extreme aerobatic maneuvering.

To top off his act, Hoover made a few last gyrations with his twin-turned-glider and then dead-sticked the silent transport to

A venerable Douglas DC-3, emblazoned in bright yellow and sporting the nickname Duggy, helped promote the world of flight on behalf of the National Aviation Hall of Fame and in 2005 was parked in the National Aviation Heritage Invitational's section at Reno. The old transport was part of a campaign to introduce children to the wonders of flying.

In 1999, the first Rolls-Royce Aviation Heritage Trophy was presented to pilot/restorer Bob Odegaard of Kindred, N.D., for his gleaming restoration of the rare Goodyear F2G-1 Super Corsair. The aircraft had been sponsored by the Standard Oil Company of Ohio (known as Sohio) in the postwar Cleveland air races. Odegaard brought the airplane back to life after it had been left to deteriorate. Interestingly, Odegaard eventually entered the beautiful racer into the modern Unlimited competition at Reno.

a greaser of a landing. But his performance did not end there. He taxied the Commander to a pre-designated spot on the ramp in front of the crowd, using only what momentum was left from his airborne maneuvering. Unbelievably, he aced the routine every time regardless of wind, density altitude, runway grade, and so on. It was a feat of virtuosity that reinforced Jimmy Doolittle's claim that Bob Hoover was the best stick-and-rudder man in the world. It is no wonder that Hoover was often called the "Great One."

Among the air show favorites is the wingwalking act. It is one thing for a skilled pilot to combine complex aerobatic maneuvers with a machine-like symmetry. It is quite another proposition to guide a beefed-up biplane through extreme

pirouettes while another person clings to the upper wing in the three dimensions of the wide-open sky.

Pilot/wingwalker pairs like Gene Soucy and Teresa Stokes make the fans feel as if they are getting an extra treat, because in addition to the impressive aerobatic routine, which could serve as an air show act of its own, there is the thrill of someone changing positions and poses in midair outside the safety of the airplane's cockpit. Enhancing the excitement is the brutish growl of the powerful radial engine, audible from any corner of the air show box. Further titillating the senses is the monstrous biplane itself, an old cropduster that seems to be constantly laboring to counteract the extra weight and drag of the intrepid soul exposed to the slipstream, while squirting a puffy line of white smoke against the unblemished drape of blue sky.

For sheer noise nothing beats the modern military jets, which turn heads every time their pilots kick in afterburner. Sometimes Reno draws strike fighters from the nearby naval air station at Fallon. When the Boeing F/A-18 Hornets or Super Hornets, decorated in either desert camouflage or aggressor blue, make their low-level passes the chit-chatter on the ground suddenly comes to a halt; it would be senseless to try to talk over the roar.

Fortunately, there is a dedicated area at the east end of the ramp where these and other military aircraft can park for the duration of the air races so that attendees have the chance to view the heavy iron up close. Reno arranges an extensive collection of contemporary military aircraft types each year. For the several days of the official racing, the east ramp is typically host to everything from tankers to fighters and jammers to transports. In 2006, the Air Force put a Predator unmanned aerial vehicle on exhibit. The best part is that pilots and the ground crews ordinarily stand by their aircraft and answer any questions not involving classified information.

Another section of the east ramp is set aside for the consistently outstanding antiques participating in the National Aviation Heritage Invitational, a competition aimed at fostering the preservation of airplanes from aviation's past. This gathering of some of the most fastidiously restored airplanes in the world makes race week worthwhile all by itself. In a given year, there may be a Travel Air, Jenny, Spartan Executive, Beech 18, Lockheed 12, Stearman, or Cub among a variety of warbirds.

All are immaculate. In fact, one has to doubt whether these gems looked as good the day they first rolled out of the factory and took to the sky. In all likelihood, the manufacturers did not show as much attention to detail as the perfectionists who give these show planes added luster when renewing their lease on airworthiness.

Piper Cubs, as aptly represented by this stunning example in the cluster of National Aviation Heritage Invitational aircraft at Reno in 2006, taught a whole generation of aspiring pilots how to fly. There is a soft spot in flyers' hearts for the little yellow airplanes that emanated from William Piper's Lock Haven, Penn. plant. This Cub's presence at Reno served to remind patrons of the diminutive classic's profound impact on aviation.

This Waco biplane is indicative of the superb restorations gracing the Reno ramp as part of the National Aviation Heritage Invitational. The fire engine red with black trim paint scheme evoked a sense of the Golden Age of Flight, when brilliantly hued biplanes at county fairs and air meets touched the imagination of a receptive public and sparked a collective love affair with aviation.

Luckily, the owners are usually on hand so that wandering spectators can satisfy their curiosity about the minute details of the restorations. While assimilating what could easily constitute sensory overload with so many stunners on the ramp, patrons have the opportunity to educate themselves about various slices of aviation's past. The rare airplanes, more likely to be seen in history books than in person, shimmer in their deserved glory under the sun.

The highlight of the air show portion of Reno's crammed schedule is a performance by a military jet team. With but a few exceptions, every year the event's organizers arrange for such a team, and sometimes Reno lucks out and gets two. When the Thunderbirds come, they do not park at Reno Stead Airport, but rather overnight on the ramp at the commercial airport in town, Reno Tahoe International, which has an Air National Guard facility that can provide round-the-clock security, fuel, and other services.

The three North American military jet demonstration squadrons—the Air Force Thunderbirds, Navy Blue Angels, and Canadian Forces Snowbirds—represent the best in air show flying. To begin with, they are teams, which means there will be formation flying—up to six aircraft at once in the case of the U.S. teams and nine in the case of the Snowbirds. Second, they fly jets. The U.S. teams show off the Air Force F-16 Fighting Falcon and the Navy F/A-18 Hornet while the Canadian team operates a trainer type, the Canadair CT-114 Tutor. Third, the teams' choreography exudes the joy of flight.

The ingredients that go into making such displays the most watched air show acts are apparent during the tuck-under rolls and the echelon breaks. Practice, skill, teamwork, pride, and determination are woven into each display. While blazing along at around 500 mph in the case of the U.S. teams, the jets are positioned no more than three feet laterally from wingtip to wingtip, which requires mutual trust on an exalted scale.

At the start of its routine, the jet team zooms overhead in a majestic full-up "Vee" formation, spitting smoke and thunder. At that juncture, the crowd can be relied on to push up against the show line rope. The jets cavort in the sky with seeming effortlessness, and we who observe from the ground are left to wonder how humans can maintain such symmetry when it looks like only machines, some kind of ultra-computerized robotons, could possibly hold all airplanes together as one like that.

The rationale for maintaining these teams with their considerable budgets usually gets reduced to the value of the performances in recruiting volunteers for the armed forces. Yes, this purpose is definitely served, and there is the less obvious but no less important factor of setting a high internal standard for currently serving pilots and maintainers with the possibility that they may advance to that highest of levels if they prove themselves worthy.

Most people who come to see the teams perform are not, however, contemplating enlistment. There is a transcendent allure. The teams exemplify what is best in flyers. As ambassadors of their respective military services, they reflect the values that are essential to the defense of liberty. Like their comrades in arms, they have inherited a towering legacy, which they perpetuate in a way that would make their military predecessors extremely proud.

When the covey of jets bursts into the beckoning blue of an afternoon sky, they touch us all, especially the young, by igniting the imagination with the wonder and the magic of flight. Every time they perform, they show us not what we are, but what we can be.

These doyens of the air are keepers of the dream that gives us cause to believe that we too can climb the mountain, rise to new heights, and find the light to be our best. Because of them, their empirical excellence that stretches to the limits of human endeavor, we know that hope is not an elusive or idle ambition, but worthwhile as nourishment for the soul.

The air show performances at the Reno air races are consistently among the best anywhere in the world. David Martin, inspired by his grandfather, who was a barnstormer, started flying as a teenager and then got the privilege of learning aerobatics from the all-time master, the late Duane Cole. Martin is at the top of his game, wowing audiences with a mesmerizing routine in a French CAP 232 carrying the colors of his corporate sponsor. Breitling is also a major sponsor of the Reno air races.

The easternmost edge of the Reno ramp is reserved for the military static display. Usually, each of the services is represented and the patrons get to walk around everything from Army helicopters, to Navy attack jets, to Air Force refuelers, to Marine transports. This Air Force F-16 Fighting Falcon is on static display with an inert AIM-9 Sidewinder air-to-air missile.

A notable contrast to the roar-and-whirl routines of most air show performers, Kent Pietsch flies a little puddle jumper from the bygone days. Hardly audible in flight, his 1942 Interstate Cadet, which many people mistake for the more familiar Piper Cub, lacks the power and aerodynamics of the hard-charging aerobatic platforms used by the other Reno acts. Pietsch is best known for his stunt of taking off and landing on the roof of a recreational vehicle. Here, he has slowed down as the RV speeds along, and at the right moment, when the two machines are in sync, he makes contact and quickly pushes forward on the control stick to keep the Cadet in place.

Engine off and safely afoot on the roof of the RV, Kent Pietsch waves an orange shirt with the number "3" in homage to the fans in Section 3. Such gestures are sure to elicit extra-loud cheers followed by rhythmic air horn toots.

Gene Soucy and Teresa Stokes are among the most recognizable performers on the air show circuit, having flown their wing-walking act together since 1988. Soucy spent 25 years as a member of the three-ship Eagles aerobatic team and won accolades at national aerobatic contests. Stokes, waving to the crowd from the upper wing of the modified Grumman Agcat, is herself an accomplished pilot. She also is a talented aviation artist.

The big biplane, which has been renamed the Showcat, lets out a throaty growl as it passes show center spewing a plume of white smoke for definition against Reno's crisp blue sky. Stokes holds on as Soucy reefs the ship over on its side at the start of a dramatic aileron roll.

To instill a greater sense of the contributions made in the defense of freedom by past and current generations of Americans in the military services, the Air Force established its Heritage Flight program and the Navy its counterpart, the Legacy Flight program. These specially choreographed formation flights occur against the backdrop of patriotic music and narration. As this World War II-era P-51 Mustang rolled down the runway for takeoff as part of a Heritage Flight formation, a boy sitting close to the show line rope stood up, without adult prompting, and raised his hand in salute. The youngster held his hand up to his brow until the old fighter passed.

The unlikely formation of prop jobs mixed with jets is the unique aspect of Air Force Heritage Flights. Here two North American P-51 Mustangs of World War II vintage fly lead and tail-end charlie with a modern Boeing F-15 Eagle and Vietnam War-era McDonnell Douglas F-4 Phantom II as wingmen. Typically, the formation makes several passes from different directions, giving the crowd an opportunity to see each aircraft from a different perspective.

The Canadian Forces Snowbirds can always be counted on to give a graceful performance in their nine Canadair CT-114 Tutor trainers. Based in Moose Jaw, Saskatchewan, the team appreciates the opportunity to visit a usually warm Reno. Here all nine aircraft are seen approaching with most trailing smoke to mark their exacting tolerances.

The Snowbirds make a knife-edge pass in unison. Nine-ship formation maneuvers require extreme coordination. Note how equidistant the aircraft are from one another. That precision happens only because of the pilots' supreme skill and dedication along with their long hours of practice.

The U.S. Air Force Thunderbirds performed at the first Reno air races in 1964 and have returned periodically in subsequent years. Flying six Lockheed Martin F-16C front-line fighters, the team exudes the core values and competencies of the Air Force. The white overhead planform of each jet silhouetted against the desert's crystalline sky and smoke trails delineating their nearly perfect trajectories make for a most exotic ballet.

After each rousing flying display or nail-biting pylon heat, the air show performers and winning racing pilots, along with their crews, are paraded up and down the show line in front of the adoring spectators in a sparkling old fire truck, prone to backfire and belch black smoke. It is a respite of sorts for the pilots. During their ride they can relax by soaking up the applause while somebody else does the driving.

CHAPTER THREE

LITTLE, LEAN, LIGHT, AND TURBINE: OFF-THE-SHELF RACERS AND HYBRIDS ON A BUDGET

ir racing classes; they are among the oldest and they are the newest. The Formula One and Biplane classes have been racing at Reno since the beginning in 1964. By contrast, the Sport and Jet classes are newcomers. Sport appeared on the scene in 1998 and Jet arrived in 2002.

Ordinarily, these classes do not receive the most media attention, nor do they come close to matching the purse of the granddaddy of air racing classes, the Unlimited class. The racers in these four classes are not the biggest, noisiest, or fastest, but they have their separate and very intense followings. Moreover, the participants demonstrate an unsurpassed passion.

The characteristic that most conspicuously distinguishes these racers from the airplanes in the two remaining classes is simply that none are from the World War II era. Also, instead of being powered by monstrous radial or V-12 piston engines, they rely on smaller, non-military piston engines or, in the case of the jets, turbine powerplants.

Except for the aircraft of the Jet class, the racers in each of these classes are sheltered in hangars during race week. The Formula One and Biplane racers share a cavernous hangar. Four dozen of these tiny airplanes are squeezed together each night, fostering a greater intermingling between the pilots and crews of different classes than anywhere else on the airport's grounds.

Sport-class aircraft, all of which are derived from marketable kits, share space in two hangars located apart from each other on the far west ramp. The Jet class, which is comparatively small, has its aircraft arrayed in rows adjoining the Unlimited racers on the east edge of the pit area.

The scattered locations of these four classes of racers, most far from the main entrance, do not deter their enthusiasts from finding them. Whether one's interest is in featherweight hybrids, spunky little biplanes, modern kit-built hotrods, or high-performance trainer jets, the common denominator is the warmth exuded by the stewards of these specialized racers. It makes the wandering from the concession stands through the pits to the distant ramp and hangars worth every step.

Out of the Box and onto the Course

Like many things, even air racing is at risk of becoming stale. Air racing organizers have tried over the years to freshen up the sport by experimenting with whole new groupings of racers centered around such aircraft as MD-500 helicopters and T-28 military trainers. There is even an effort underway as this is written to create a category of rocket-propelled racers. Once in a while, the trial of a new class of racers clicks and the roster of longstanding stalwarts is joined, giving the air races an infusion of new blood.

One of the success stories is the Sport class. Sport racers, powered by reciprocating engines with displacements no larger than 650 cubic inches and capable of minimum qualifying speeds of 200 mph, have been competing at Reno ever since. The establishment of this class recognized the emergence of a corner of the kitplane market that thrived on high performance and that enjoyed widespread popularity.

The larger investment is in time and labor, but those who make the plunge tend to find the building process invigorating. At the end they can relish the fact that they were the ones who brought the airplane to fruition. The finished product occupies a place in the sky because of their handiwork. The long hours toiling on the construction quite justifiably stir an inner pride. Not all of the race pilots build the aircraft they fly, but in every case there is an appreciation for the craftsman who did.

Building the racers from kits instills an intimate understanding of the aircraft systems. All pilots must know their equipment, and the kitbuilders have a head start on their flying brethren because of the hands-on experience they gain in putting the pieces together. The tension settings for pulleys and cables, the mating of carbon-derived fuselage sections, the landing gear wheel alignment, and a slew of other considerations are not mere abstractions but real-world issues for the kitbuilders.

At one time, kitbuilding was a cottage industry. The Experimental Aircraft Association, founded in Paul and Audrey Pobereznys' basement in the early 1950s, had, at its

Opposite: Tim Bovee, a truck mechanic from East Wenatchee, Wash., used to fly this yellow- and blue-trimmed Midget Mustang, race 90, Purty Pony, *in the Formula One races. Not quite as streamlined as the Cassutts, it nevertheless could hold its own in the less demanding heats. In 2002, Bovee led the first few laps of the Formula One Bronze race, but ended up trailing three Cassutts with an average speed of 185.359 mph.*

The night before a race is not necessarily spent partying at the casinos in downtown Reno. Many of the pilots and their crews hunch over their aircraft trying to tweak an engine or correct a mechanical problem, sometimes into the late hours of the evening. Some observers have remarked that the races are won on the ground in the preparations. This Lancair Legacy, race 2, Modo Mio, owned by Vince Walker of Boulder, Colo., received attention to its composite surfaces as the sun was setting after a long day of racing. Walker piloted his airplane to a third-place finish in the Sport class Silver race in 2006.

heart, the avid hobbyists who loved tinkering in their hangars at local airports, carefully crafting small, flyable airplanes. It was a reflection of the organization's origins that the word "Experimental" figured so prominently in its name.

Kitbuilt aficionados found that they could produce, albeit on a one-at-a-time basis, aircraft that more closely fit their specific needs and desires. Their planes might be made to go faster, or perhaps cover greater distance for less fuel than the mass-produced models coming from general aviation's big three—Cessna, Piper, and Beech. Some enterprising entrepreneurs saw a market. The ingenious aeronautical maverick Burt Rutan—known now for his futuristic airplane design that circumnavigated the globe on a single tank of fuel and for his nascent exoatmospheric tourism project, which has involved a prototype spaceship that actually ascended to the edge of space—ventured into the plans-built sector, fostering a whole family of individually assembled and distinctive-looking canard-wing airplanes.

As the field matured, other ambitious visionaries decided to offer not just the blueprints but the parts. The key, the lure, was a sleek new appearance, something different from the staid designs of the big three's plants in Wichita and Vero Beach, coupled with performance that bettered what the established industry players were producing. Aviation's entrenched old guard, manufacturers that had given the flying fraternity such revered aircraft as the Cub, the Skyhawk, and the Bonanza, seemed to be resting on their laurels, stagnant in the face of promising new technologies. There was an opportunity, a void that could be filled. Starting in the late 1980s, when composites were first becoming a possible new material for use in aircraft construction, a handful of imaginative individuals decided to try their hand at modernizing the industry by providing pilots with alternatives to the old standbys. It represented a leap of faith. So much would depend on the emerging science of composites, which, in theory, promised greater strength, lower weight, and competitive cost in relation to conventional materials. Also, the forward-leaning entrepreneurs sought to achieve significant performance improvements through attractive, clean-sheet designs that incorporated aerodynamic streamlining. The marketplace would serve as the ultimate arbiter for the new end products.

Each of the companies that succeeded in cultivating loyal clienteles was associated with an individual who served as the driving force. At Lancair Performance Aircraft of Redmond, Ore., the guiding light was Lance A. Neibauer. At Glasair Aviation (previously Stoddard-Hamilton) of Arlington, Wash., it was Tom Hamilton. The kitplanes that these innovators developed caught on, mushrooming into model lineups with differing performance specifications and prices to match. From their meager beginnings, these companies have evolved to the point where, as of this writing, Lancair has sold nearly 1,900 aircraft kits and Glasair a similar number.

Today, these companies have different owners. At Lancair, it is Joseph C. Bartels, a pilot and New Orleans attorney, while at Glasair, it is Thomas W. Wathen, a former chairman of Pinkerton's, who is also the owner of the well-known Flabob Airport in Riverside, Calif. Both companies are represented extensively in the Sport class with their respective designs. The Lancair Legacy and the Glasair III are the most common race entrants.

Other notable innovators have included Papa 51 Ltd., a now-defunct company that in 1995 started developing a three-quarter scale P-51 Mustang known as the "Thunder Mustang." Powered by a 640-horsepower Ryan Falconer V-12 engine (patterned after the Rolls-Royce Merlin engine), the Thunder Mustang is a peppy racer. Unfortunately, in 1998 one of the early versions of the kitplane went down, killing the pilot and passenger, which precluded further sales.

A small company, Nemesis Air Racing in Mojave, Calif., has developed an ultra-streamlined, high-tech racer that looks like it is going fast just sitting on the tarmac. The aeronautical luminary behind this futuristic racer, called the Nemesis NXT, is 11-time Formula One champion Jon Sharp. An engineer at the cutting-edge Lockheed Martin Skunk Works, Sharp and his wife Patricia oversee a small, motivated staff noted for continually refining their company's aircraft. Because demand for such an exceptionally high-performance airplane is limited, not many of the Nemesis NXT kits have been sold. Fortunately, the Sport class rules require that only five kits have to have been delivered in order for the design to be accepted for competition at the Reno air races.

A Sport racer that is not exactly a purebred comes from John Harmon's Bakersfield, Calif., operation. The various versions of the Harmon Rocket are converted from the line of

For safety reasons, no aircraft can start up except when on the open apron opposite the pit area. Sport class racers must be towed or pulled from their two designated hangars and then back again. Here, Pete Zaccagnino's Lancair IV, race 28, is shown on its way back to one of the hangars following a heat. This aircraft came in fourth place in the 2006 Sport class Silver race.

San Diego resident David Sterling's Lancair Legacy, race 8, is being pulled into one of the Sport-class hangars made available during race week at Reno. The hangar provides welcome shelter from the elements, especially the desert winds that can develop into dangerously strong gales in the late afternoon.

The North American P-51 Mustang was one of the leading fighters of World War II and is one of the best performing piston-powered airplanes ever built. The Thunder Mustang is a kit design that takes the basic shell of the original P-51 design and scales it down, creating a more modern, lower-cost Mustang. Accordingly, the Thunder Mustang is a logical Sport class platform. John Parker, seen here taxiing his race 351, Blue Thunder, is a serious contender for top honors. With an average speed of 350.340 mph in 2006, he came in third place in the Sport Gold race. He almost certainly would have done even better if his aircraft's supercharger system had not malfunctioned, causing the Falconer V-12 engine to suffer a drop in horsepower.

Aeronautical engineer
Jon Sharp, whose industry experience includes working
for the always forward-leaning Lockheed Martin Skunk Works, is recognized as one of the
outstanding innovators in modern air racing. His Nemesis racer, which he designed and built for Formula One racing, dom-
inated the field for nine years. Sharp decided to take on the new challenge of competing in the faster Sport class. He designed
a kit version of a souped-up Nemesis, which he calls Nemesis NXT. For sheer streamlining there is nothing like it. The aircraft is
more a finely sculpted toothpick than a bullet. The composite fuselage is mated to a special TSIO-540-NXT engine developed for
Sharp by Lycoming. Flying his creation at the 2006 air races, Sharp captured first place in the Sport Gold with an average speed
of 360.389 mph. This angle shows the unconventional scimitar-style propeller blades of Jon Sharp's sleek race 3X, Nemesis NXT.
Note the near absence of drag-inducing bulges, protrusions, or fairings at any place behind the cowling.

Van's RV aircraft, one- or two-seat taildraggers that are appealingly economical kitplanes. Harmon has used his extensive flying background of more than 6,000 hours as a military and developmental test pilot to place in the Sport class' Silver races, but in recent years his entries have been superseded by the more exotic designs. About 100 of his conversion kits have been sold and built.

A few other types round out the field. There is the diminutive Questair Venture, which has a pod-on-the-wing appearance. A customized White Lightning, resembling a modish Piper Comanche, features a tail-mounted supercharger that doubles the engine's horsepower. The straight-

forward Swearingen SX 300 has been around for a while and it remains competitive.

The Sport class is leading the way with newfangled engine and aerodynamic technologies. Some large corporate entities, like Lycoming, are involved with certain racing teams because they see an opportunity for their businesses to benefit from the advances being fostered. Also, there is the potential for stamping the corporate logo on any successes, gaining promotional value.

Still, at its core, the Sport class is the realm of the entrepreneur. In hangars at general aviation airports, bare-bones teams, long on ideas, enthusiasm, and dedication—even if

One of the under-reported aspects of the Reno air races is the clockwork coordination on the ramp and in the air. The flying-related activities during race week unfold with a precision that rivals even that of the military. Making operations flow seamlessly is a credit to the organizational talents of the air race officials and the professionalism of the racing pilots and their crews. Before every Sport class race, the aircraft are aligned on the ramp. They taxi out, take off in sequence, and then, once airborne, join up in loose formation for an air start. Each activity during the day is allocated a time slot and, despite occasional glitches, the program usually proceeds within an acceptable margin of the formal schedule.

short of financial resources, conjure up improvements that have resulted in an almost unbroken progression of increasing speeds on the Reno race course. Absolute world speed records are not being set, but component breakthroughs and pinpoint refinements keep arising from the cramped workshops and improvised laboratories of these inventive aviators. They embody the spirit of the earliest air races. Through their dedication, the members of the Sport class perpetuate the proud legacy of the Cleveland air races.

Eclectic Racers

The term "midget racer" is almost an oxymoron because the first instinct in visualizing a racing plane is to think of a monstrous machine that stands high off the ground bristling with big-bore cylinders. Yet in the history of air racing there has been a recurring difference of opinion as to whether *might* or *light* should be the preferred design driver.

In the heyday of the 1930s, Steve Wittman pioneered scaled-down racers, deliberately trading away heft and power for reductions in weight and drag with racers like his home-built *Chief Oshkosh*. The fact was that at the time liquid-cooled engines tended to be disadvantageous for civilian racing planes because of their complexity.

Nevertheless, displaying his predilection for nonconformity, Wittman himself fitted a Curtiss D-12 liquid-cooled engine to his tiny *Bonzo* for racing at Cleveland in 1935. An

overheating problem with that engine caused Wittman to fall from the lead in the Thompson Trophy race and finish second, perhaps unwittingly supporting his own philosophy of keeping racers spare and slender.

Recognizing that most of the little planes simply did not have the brawn to compete effectively against the beastly racers in the premier Thompson Trophy contests, and that Depression-era economics dampened the ability of many would-be participants to develop big racing planes, the Cleveland air races encouraged builders with varying levels of resources by hosting racing categories limited to aircraft whose engines did not exceed a specified displacement. The most important of these was the Greve Trophy race, which became an annual event starting in 1934.

Underwritten by Louis W. Greve, who headed the Cleveland Pneumatic Tool Co., this race was restricted to airplanes with engines having a displacement of 550 cubic inches. Almost all the racers in this field used some variant of the Menasco engine. Exceptions included Steve Wittman, who raced with a Cirrus engine, and Frenchman Michel Detroyat, whose Caudron C-460 had a Renault Bengali engine.

Tony LeVier in the Schoenfeldt-Rider R-4 *Firecracker* and Art Chester in his *Goon*, respectively, closed out the pre-World War II period with new records in the 1938 and 1939 Greve Trophy races. Interestingly, the Menasco-powered *Firecracker*, which excelled among the 550-cubic inch racers, also was competitive in the last Thompson Trophy race, nearly snatching a

Earl Hibler of Alameda, Calif., has been a regular Sport class competitor in his race 40, Baby Doll, *a Glasair II. By contemporary standards this mid-1990s aircraft with fixed-landing gear has been superseded by newer, cleaner designs that, among other things, have retractable landing gear. Nevertheless, the aircraft can be counted on to put in a gutsy performance with Hibler at the controls. In fact, race 40 was a very respectable third in the 2006 Sport Bronze race with an average speed of 268.399 mph.*

win from Roscoe Turner in his Laird-Turner racer powered by a 1,830-cubic-inch Pratt & Whitney Wasp Sr. radial engine.

When the Cleveland air races resumed after the war, all five types of racers in the field of 10 Thompson Trophy finishers were frontline fighters of World War II vintage—the Bell P-39 Airacobra, the Bell P-63 King Cobra, the Lockheed P-38 Lightning, the North American P-51 Mustang, and the Goodyear FG-1 Corsair. These aircraft were a far cry from the top racers of just seven years earlier; speeds in the Thompson Trophy races escalated dramatically and a new bar was set.

At the time, there was not much point in individuals, no matter how talented, trying to develop competing or near-competing piston racers in their backyards and garages for the Thompson Trophy races, which were by then dominated by the major players in the aviation industry. But pilots without much money or lavish sponsorship still yearned to participate in the sport. You could come to the races with your airplane, and there would be an opening somewhere in the week's activities. The fact that you might not compete against the top-notch racers was okay; you could at least be racing.

Accordingly, in 1947, the second year of the postwar air races, a new class was established with the input of the Professional Race Pilots Association, whose leaders had begun to envision such a class in the late 1930s. The new class was based around the Continental Motors C-85 engine, a four-cylinder, air-cooled engine with a 188-cubic inch displacement. The rules limited these midgets to engines with a maximum displacement of 190 cubic inches. Fortuitously, Goodyear Tire agreed to sponsor a marquee race for this new class during the annual National Air Races at Cleveland.

For three years, Cleveland hosted the Goodyear Trophy race. As might have been expected, the key competitors included some of the old hands from the pre-War Greve Trophy races. Though winning speeds never approached 200 mph, Steve Wittman, Tony LeVier, and Art Chester were in their element flying homebuilt racers at Cleveland.

Starting in 1948, Continental Motors decided to get in on the action and so it underwrote a series of midget races that lasted for five years. Known as the Continental Motors races, these contests applied the same requirements that

The most common types in the Sport class are Lancairs and Glasairs. These two kit-built aircraft are readily available and they provide their owners with high performance at relatively low cost. When the Sport-class races began at Reno in 1998, the paint schemes on these racers were predictably prosaic, but over time they have slowly begun to mirror the flashiness of their cousins in the other classes. This is a Lancair 360, race 4, Unleashed, owned by Airbus A-320 pilot Scott Germain of Phoenix, Ariz. Germain's Lancair is the only Sport class racer equipped with a four-cylinder engine, the Superior XP-400. The smaller engine reflects industry's interest in using the relatively new Sport class races to develop and improve economically viable products for the general aviation market.

held sway for the Goodyear Trophy races. All competing racers used Continental's small but reliable engine. The aircraft had to have fixed landing gear and employ fixed-pitch propellers.

The first three Continental Motors races occurred in Miami, and the final two took place near Detroit. Predictably Steve Wittman and his friend, William Brennand, raced in these contests. By the end of the series in 1951, winning race speeds had steadily climbed to just short of 200 mph.

With the passage of time, Continental Motors discontinued production of its 188-cubic inch engine. This necessitated a change in the rules, and in 1968 the maximum allowable engine displacement was raised slightly to 200 cubic inches. Racers began using the 100-horsepower Continental Motors O-200 engine, and winning speeds soon shot up from prior

levels. Other requirements remained unchanged. Aircraft in the class had to continue to weigh at least 500 pounds and have a wing surface area of at least 66 square feet. At the same time, the class that had been referred to variously as the midget racers or the 190-Cubic Inch class became known as the Formula One class.

Formula One racers, though tiny in physical dimension, are large in stature. As in the past, today's small racing planes are a real-world laboratory of innovation, albeit within the class' parameters. Like the aircraft of the Sport class, these racers enjoy a grassroots appeal. They bring the sport of air racing within reach of those with limited resources. Being built from scratch quite naturally makes the Formula One class a favorite of the homebuilt movement that comprises the core of the Experimental Aircraft Association's 170,000 members. These airplanes, their builders, pilots, and crews speak to the heart of everyday flyers at local airports.

The diminutive Formula One racers stand out in the rainbow of colors they present against the neutral palettes of the Reno sky and desert. Vibrant yellow, midnight blue, charcoal black, snowflake white, two-tone, checkerboard, stenciled, and ornamental schemes embellish the sky.

The field of Formula One racers consists primarily of aircraft based on the tried-and-true Cassutt design dating back to the 1960s. The airplanes are squat taildraggers constructed with a tubular metal frame covered by fabric to the aft and fiberglass to the nose. Notably, the racers have a fully cantilevered mid-wing. The absence of flying wires and interwing struts makes these aircraft aerodynamically cleaner than the little biplanes with which they share hangar space during race week.

In the 1990s, a new phenomenon swept the Formula One class. Jon Sharp, the Lockheed Martin Skunk Works engineer who had won in the class a couple of times in the 1980s, introduced his clean-sheet design which he called *Nemesis*. Radical in appearance, the new Formula One racer was destined to win nine championships with Sharp himself at the controls. Only Ray Cote, flying a variety of racers over the years, won more Formula One Gold races an amazing total of 13. Eventually, Sharp's racer was retired to the Smithsonian Institution's National Air and Space Museum, which is a testament to the airplane's influence on air racing.

As undeniably invincible as Sharp was during the 1990s, *Nemesis* was surpassed in 2006 by Gary Hubler's extremely modified Cassutt, *Mariah*, race 95. Hubler established a new class record with an average speed of 257.047 mph in the 2006 Formula One Gold race. It was his fifth straight win in his constantly evolving old Cassutt. (It should be noted that Jon Sharp and *Nemesis* still hold the Formula One Class qualifying speed record of 263.188 mph, set on Sept. 13, 1999.)

Built in 1972, *Mariah* was raced that very year at Reno, though under a different name. It went through several owners and even incurred substantial damage in a 1980 crackup. Hubler and a partner began a laborious reconstruction that became the racer's transformation.

Mariah looks markedly different from the more or less stock Cassutt racers at Reno. The tail surfaces and cockpit

This Glasair III, race 10, Warp Speed Wanda, belongs to Mike Jones of Fullerton, Calif. In 2006, Jones made an impressive showing with a second-place finish in the Sport Silver race.

Although the Sport class racers remain clustered for part of the first lap after their air start, they soon scatter as the performance differentials and variances in pilot technique manifest themselves. Note the participation of the canard-equipped VariEze in the middle of the frame. Such Rutan-inspired designs are not common in the Sport class as Lancairs and Glasairs have become the favored aircraft in this category of racing.

This is the view from the grandstands as Sport class racers vie for position passing over the home pylon at show center. The kit-built airplanes sometimes reach a speed of slightly more than 400 mph on the six laps of the normal 6.368-mile course, which expands to 8.372 miles for the Sport Gold race.

Mornings start early for the Formula One pilots and crews. Usually, the lightweight Formula One racers are the first to get airborne at the Reno air races. The order of flying is simple. The winds almost always kick up as the day wears on, so the tiny airplanes that can barely fit a normal-size person are shown appropriate deference. The ritual commences at dawn, when the hangar doors crack open, permitting the sun's still-horizontal rays to flood the hangar. Here, pilot Jay Jones of Buena Vista, Colo., and his crew guide a Cassutt III M, race 45, Quadnickel, from the hangar as the ramp comes to life in preparation for the first race of the day. Quadnickel won the Formula One Bronze race with an average speed of 225.028 mph.

canopy have different shapes and the wing is made of composites. With a consistent lead over the competition for five years running, Hubler may be on track to match or even supersede the dominance of past class champions Jon Sharp and Ray Cote.

The Formula One racers could have just stagnated over time. After all, the governing rules are rather onerous. Yet, the relatively recent crop of pilots drawn to Formula One planes, not unlike certain young men at Cleveland at an earlier time, saw opportunities for refinement that might improve performance. Refusing to accept things as they are and imagining a better way is where this process starts. Then it becomes a matter of implementing the envisaged enhancements, perspiration following the inspiration.

The ultimate proving ground, the acid test, is found on the race course amid the other airplanes and before the

intensively focused eyes of thousands of spectators. In the cockpit, however, flying the airplane takes precedence. Once the flying starts, all the rest becomes subordinate and is shifted into the periphery. A year's worth of preparation—fine-tuning the engine to a sonorous purr, polishing the leading edge of the wing to a glistening finish, and, lastly, taping over gaps in the cracks between the canopy ledge and the fuselage while awaiting the flagman's signal—will be consumed in the flash of about eight frantic minutes swirling around the designated pylons.

From the grandstands, the racers are almost like self-propelled arrows lunging forward in quick spurts. From the cockpit, the view is of a stark horizon with a brownish landscape below and a sparkling blue sky above, like a video game or the projection screen of a flight simulator, only you are skimming over the ground at breakneck speed. If it were

The Formula One pilots and crews huddle for an impromptu briefing. Even on days when the afternoon thermometer readings reach well into the 80s, September mornings at mile-high Reno can be nippy. Old hands know to come attired for the elements. The mood on the pavement far removed from the blaring commentary of the air show announcers and the familiar scent of cotton candy that wafts over the show line ramp is genial but tense. Teams have come from around the country for their few minutes on this course, and they intend to do their best.

possible to see the spectacle from above, high over the great basin that accommodates the race, it likely would reveal a series of graceful orbits, humankind in resplendent harmony with the natural environment, striving without presumption to go in circles, yes, but to end up somewhere new, pure, and gratifying.

Double-Decker Bantams

Biplanes are not new to air racing. Indeed, the earliest air races featured many biplanes. But the design elements that made the biplane so appealing as a basic flying machine militated against its fortunes as a racing platform. Even by the time of the air meet at Reims in 1909, monoplanes were entered and were considered the leading contenders.

The biplane configuration offers the ruggedness of truss construction as well as the safety, depending on spacing and stagger, of a primitive form of stall warning whereby one wing stalls before the other. Yet, these laudatory features that emanate from the double-wing design are drawbacks for racing

purposes because the extra wing with the typical bracing struts and wires poses additional weight and drag. Not surprisingly, outside of the Biplane class, all the entrants in Reno's races are monoplanes.

Despite the inherent drawbacks of the biplane racer, there is a soft spot in every aviator's heart for biplanes. Not only was the very first successful powered airplane designed with two wings, but for years after the Wright Flyer took to the skies, biplanes served as pursuit ships, exhibition aircraft, and commercial transports. Sopwith Camels and Fokker D VIIs, combat biplanes, dueled in aerial dogfights during World War I, forging the mystique of the fighter ace. Curtiss JN-4 Jennies taught a generation to fly, and then the rickety biplanes found renewed life in the captivating world of barnstorming.

As late as World War II, biplanes were used to teach Army and Navy cadets the basics of airmanship. Students climbed into the open cockpits attired in leather jackets, and, to keep the onrushing wind at bay when airborne, they pulled goggles down over their eyes and wrapped white silk scarves around

Cozy is an understatement in describing the cockpits of Formula One racers. Here, pilot Charlie Greer shoehorns himself into his Gilbert DG-1, race 69, Miss B. Haven, on the runway just minutes before the first race of the day on a typically chilly September morning in the high desert. Greer wears a parachute and, like other pilots competing in the air races, a NASCAR-style fire-retardant suit. In the 2006 air races, he placed third in the Formula One Gold race with an average speed of 247.356 mph.

their necks. This was a period that reinforced the image of the aviator as a gallant and daring fellow. In fact, when air racing was reborn at Reno in 1964, the various racing classes included one dedicated to that most ubiquitous of World War II biplane trainers, the immortal Boeing Stearman.

Alas, the Stearman's fat wings, labyrinth of struts, criss-crossing flying wires, and flatiron radial engine hold it from cruising much above 100 mph. Even when the type's stock 220-horsepower Continental engine was replaced with the 450-horsepower Pratt & Whitney engine, the increase in speed was only modest. The cumbrous wood-and-fabric trainer was not really a racing plane, and predictably the type was not raced at Reno again. But biplanes had evolved since the time of the big radial-engine trainers.

Conceived as superior aerobatic platforms, petite biplanes filled an important niche in sport aviation. Because of their lightweight, reduced frontal cross-section, and comparatively high thrust-to-weight ratio, these newer biplanes offered speed on a level that far exceeded the performance of

the leaden clunkers that preceded them. Accordingly, there was a way for air racing to preserve the romance of the biplane.

Rules were adopted to keep the Biplane class competitive. Standards were formulated around the design characteristics of the Pitts S-1, the aerobatic classic. With this widely used aircraft as the core of the class, there would be no doubt that the annual heats had sufficient numbers of contestants. Limitations include a cap on engine displacement of 360-cubic inches. Moreover, each racer has to have non-retractable landing gear and fixed-pitch propellers. Overall wing area is restricted to 75-square feet with a further curb on the variance in sizes of the upper and lower wings.

These rules do not allow for much innovation. From the early 1970s until the late 1990s, the top speeds in the Biplane class had essentially maxed out in the high-190 mph to low-200 mph range. In 1996, aerobatic flight instructor Patti Johnson-Nelson piloted her Mong Sport biplane, *Full Tilt Boogie*, race number 40, to 212.811 mph, which represented

From the cockpit of his GR-7 Panther, race 87, Madness, pilot Steve Temple gestures to one of his crewmen during the last round of preflight checks as the countdown to the scheduled start of the air race is well underway. Verbal communication becomes difficult as pilots and crews prepare to crank the racers' engines. Pilots have hearing protection stuffed in their ears, and besides, any shouted instructions might be confused with words floating across the runway from teams setting up nearby. Communication for Formula One teams readying for the start of a race is reduced to simple hand signals.

a new milestone for the class. However, it was not until the new millennium that the Biplane class' winning speeds exceeded that level.

The Biplane class has evolved to where all but a few of the entered aircraft are the Pitts S-1 type. There remains just a sprinkling of other types, such as the Mong Sport Biplane, which is still competitive, and the Smith Miniplane, which is not.

Despite the considerable limitations on modifying racers in the class, a notable breakthrough has been achieved by Tom Aberle of Fallbrook, Calif. He has applied his creative energies to squeeze a lot more performance out of the Mong design with *Full Tilt Boogie*. He sold the racer to Patti Johnson-Nelson, who achieved three impressive wins with it.

In more recent times, he reworked a Mong's empennage and reshaped its vertical stabilizer and rudder, reducing drag. In addition, he installed novel propellers (first a three-blade and then a four-blade) designed by Paul Lipps. Aberle's racer, named *Phantom*, reached new top speeds in the Biplane Gold races in 2004, 2005, and 2006, significantly raising the prevailing average speed to 251.958 mph. This speed is actu-

ally faster than the winning speed in the 2006 T-6 Gold race, which means that the Biplane class has finally moved up from its status as the slowest class at Reno. Like Gary Hubler, Jon Sharp, and Ray Cote in the Formula One class, Aberle seems destined to dominate the Biplane class for some time.

In the face of Aberle's domination, one wonders if the class rules will be loosened to encourage more innovation. If a Mong could be so radically enhanced within the current rules, it can only be imagined how fast a competing Pitts aircraft could be with a meaningful adjustment in the severe restrictions.

In the meantime, the many essentially stock Pitts S-1s will continue to occupy the bulk of the available slots in the Biplane class. Pitts biplanes have made a lasting mark in aerobatic flying such that anything that keeps these iconic aircraft before the public eye should be welcomed.

Spawned by Curtis Pitts, the dean of post-World War II aerobatic aircraft designers, the line of biplanes bearing his name became synonymous with high-end aerobatics. Roll rate, climb performance, control response, and overall crispness of maneuvers are the hallmarks of this great aircraft.

Consequently it became the preferred choice for many leading aerobatic competitors and air show performers.

The Pitts elevated the state of the art to a new plateau. Calibrated so expertly for the aerobatic pilot, previously difficult maneuvers were turned into easily achievable ones. At the same time, the stout little biplane enabled a level of unprecedented precision in the sky and raised the bar for aerobatic performers. As the aerobatic platform of choice for many years, the type remains plentiful enough that Pitts S-1s will be available for participation in the air races into the foreseeable future.

Like the tiny racers of the Formula One class, biplane racers perform a racehorse start. Arrayed on the runway in staggered rows of three-two-three, with their positions determined by their rank in the qualifying trials, the aircraft charge along the pavement when they receive the wave of the green flag. Within moments they alight and remain low, building up speed as they head for the course.

Still clumped together when they swing into their first orbit around the pylons, the biplane racers approximate a buzzing swarm of oversized bumble bees. The sound is accentuated by a vibratory hum that comes from the air whistling through the tightly rigged inter-wing bracing wires. It is as though the tiny ships are on the attack, coming closer in ominous pursuit with their collective buzz and hum, growing ever louder and higher pitched. On their way to the westernmost pylon, the field thins out. When the racers zip past again, one can imagine that these slimmed-down biplanes are recreating an earlier era, in a sense, when different kinds of biplanes lumbered across the prairies, rousing the countryside with the magic of flight.

With each pass in front of the grandstands, the contemporary biplanes stimulate sometimes-dormant sympathies among flight enthusiasts, who remain favorably disposed to the biplane, the treasured multiple-wing configuration, inherited from aviation's illustrious past. For their part, the pilots shoehorned into the cramped cockpits of their Pitts, Mong, and Smith racers dashing around the pylons likely educe a personal rapture and jubilance. From their special vantage point, they know the joys of biplane flying.

One of the last steps before getting the green flag is fastening on the canopies over the pilots. Pilot Steve Temple flies giant C-5 Galaxy cargo planes as a major in the 445th Airlift Wing of the Air Force Reserve. When he is racing in the Formula One class at Reno he has gone from one end of the aviation spectrum to the other. Madness was fourth in the 2006 Formula One Silver race with an average speed of 227.867 mph.

One of the more colorful airplanes among the Formula One racers is pilot Brian Reberry's Cassutt III M, race 13, N-A-Rush. Like the other contenders in the early morning contest, the little purple-green-orange racer with its checkerboard rudder is aligned on runway 08, pointed directly into the sun, as crewmembers hunch over the cockpit in final preparation. Reberry took fourth place in the 2006 Formula One Bronze race with an average speed of 213.517 mph.

Light that Candle

Like biplanes, jets are not new to air racing. When the National Air Races resumed at Cleveland in 1946, jets were all the rage. A wholly new breed of aircraft capable of far greater speeds than anything that had ever been exhibited at Cleveland before was now being unveiled and demonstrated.

The new propulsive technology, the object of research in small labs in Britain and Germany during the 1930s, evolved quickly once World War II started. By the end of the war, the Germans and British had fielded operational jet fighters, the Messerschmitt Me-262 and the Gloster Meteor, respectively. America was a little slower to jump on the bandwagon. But after Bell Aircraft's attempt at developing a frontline jet based on its XP-59A lagged, the Army Air Force urgently needed to move forward with a totally new development program. The Luftwaffe's deadly jet sent shivers through the Allied high command and thus provided further impetus.

Chief of the Army Air Force, General Henry H. "Hap" Arnold, turned to the brilliant, if sometimes irascible, Clarence L. "Kelly" Johnson of Lockheed. Miraculously, within six months of the contract's signing, the company delivered its first jet. It was a beauty, elegant in its simplicity. A fuselage that took the form of a sculpted tube to house the engine was at the center of the design. Interestingly, the accomplished racing pilot Tony LeVier was a Lockheed test pilot, and he did much of the flight-testing on the prototype.

Although it was produced too late to enter combat in World War II, the P-80 Shooting Star was a hit at the first post-war air races in Cleveland. In 1946, a jet version of the Thompson Trophy Race was held. Half a dozen of the P-80s competed in a six-lap, 180-mile closed-course contest. All of the entrants were Army Air Force pilots flying military P-80s, as this was long before jets started to show up in civilian hands. Major Gus Lundquist won with an average speed of 515.9 mph in what almost qualified as a photo-finish. He was followed across the finish line no more than three seconds later by famed World War II fighter ace Major Robin Olds. There was also a cross-country Bendix race for the P-80s as well as a speed dash involving powered dives.

The Formula One racers are arrayed across the runway three abreast. This is possible since the pavement is 150-feet wide. Engines are running to warm up in the frigid morning air. When the signal is given by race officials, the ground crews will dart to the sidelines, and moments later the starter will flag the pilots to begin. Given their light weight, relative high power, and the cool ambient temperature, they will be aloft soon after starting their takeoff rolls, leaving most of the 7,600-foot runway unused.

The jet races at Cleveland continued for as long as the National Air Races hung on, but some questioned the relevance of these contests, which were limited to stock, military fighters whose performance parameters were well-known. Though there were occasional jet races following the demise of the Cleveland event, no regularly scheduled jet contests occurred again until Reno air racing officials set up an invitational race in 2002.

The success of the first few reborn jet races prompted officials to convert the Jet class into an open competition—whoever qualified in the speed trials would be included among the eight or nine available slots in the single-prize race for jets. However, to keep the new jet races truly competitive, it was decided to limit the course to one type of jet—the Aero Vodochody L-39 Albatros.

Established in 1954 as the result of the merger of two aeronautical entities (one of which had built MiG-15 fighters under license) in what is now the Czech Republic, Aero Vodochody reached its design zenith with the introduction of its L-39 jet trainer/light attack aircraft. This model first flew in 1968. Since that time, more than 3,000 units in a variety of configurations have been delivered to countries all over the world. The main customer was the Soviet Union. Other customers were spread largely throughout the Third World.

With the collapse of the Iron Curtain, the aircraft began migrating to Western locations, and are now readily available in the United States at very reasonable prices—for a high-performance jet. So many L-39s have been built that they are in ample supply. The L-39 is known for its gentle handling characteristics, ease of maintenance, and low-operating costs. For civilian pilots who want the experience of flying a fighter-like jet, the Albatros is a top choice.

When the jets are lined up on the ramp in a neat row in preparation for the Jet Gold race, they exude a simple majesty. If not for their dramatic color variations, the lineup could be mistaken for a jet squadron readying for a mission. Upon spooling up, the whine of the engines invariably draws the crowd's attention. Spectators in the pit drop what they are doing and turn their heads in the direction of the ramp.

This standard mid-wing Cassutt III M is maneuvered into an extremely steep bank as it rounds a pylon. Named Midnight Lightning and emblazoned with race number 54, it belongs to pilot Gary Davis of Sanger, Texas, who placed fifth in the 2006 Formula One Silver race with an average speed of 225.262 mph.

Everything happens fast in the jets, and not just anyone can fly in this demanding class. Pilots in the class must have at least 1,000 hours of flying time and be checked out and signed off in the L-39 specifically. Airline pilot John Penney, who started competing in an L-39 in 2005, had already accumulated substantial air racing experience as the pilot of *Rare Bear*, a winning Bearcat in past Unlimited Gold races. Dave Morss, pilot of the L-39 *Tejas Pistolaero*, has been racing for nearly three decades, with more laps circled than any other pilot since air racing began. Even the so-called rookies sometimes are nothing of the sort. Trevor Schaefer flew an L-39 for the first time in 2006, but he had flown F-15 Eagles as an Air Force fighter pilot.

The jets are not subject to drastic modification, so they are evenly matched. They swoop in from around Peavine Mountain to the south of the course looking like a highly practiced air demonstration team in near-perfect line-abreast formation. When the pace plane pulls up trailing a long plume of white smoke, the race is underway.

Aiming for the guide pylon, the L-39s start to break from formation and zoom ahead in what seems from the ground to be reckless abandon. It is a free-for-all where each jet is hot. The participants tear across the desert in their sleek jets only 50 feet above the surface. Throttled up, these speeding jet trainers make a swooshing sound as they dart past the pylons. Some of the jets are decorated in military camouflage schemes; without prior knowledge, one might think that dogfights or ground strafing were taking place.

The race never lets up. The jets jockey for position down the straight-aways and during the pylon turns. Passing can be tricky because of the jet blast of the racer in front. The air currents in the late afternoon add to the challenge—nature rattles the pilots in opposite directions as they try to keep their plane on the course line. The jets endure six laps of this at speeds approaching 500 mph without any slacking off. One lucky pilot pulls ahead of the pack to whiz past the checkered flag at the home pylon.

The Jet class is the newest addition to the Reno air races. It showcases an entirely different type of airplane from what Reno audiences had been accustomed to seeing in the pylon races, yet is a type that first appeared on the racing circuit after World War II. By returning to the past, the Reno air races have entered the future, keeping the races exciting for the regulars and the newcomers alike. The jets look like they are here to stay.

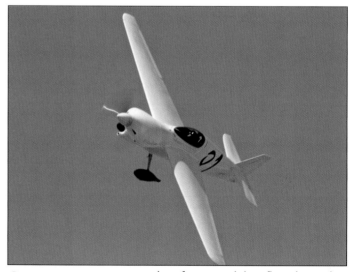

Computer engineer Ray Debs of Boise, Idaho, flew this Debs-Weinman 001, race 81, Carbon Slipper, to fifth place in the 2006 Formula One Gold race. That was a very impressive showing given the caliber of the competition. His average speed was 231.069 mph. This aircraft is notable for its lack of color.

The dominator of the Formula One air races in the new century has been Caldwell, Idaho-pilot Gary Hubler. He has flown this Cassutt III M, race 95, Mariah, to first-place wins of the Formula One Gold races every year from 2002 to 2006. Observers believe it is possible that he will have a long run at the top, comparable to the earlier runs of Ray Cote and Jon Sharp. He zipped around the 3.1875-mile course with an average speed of 257.047 mph, setting a new course record.

Another Formula One Gold race qualifier is pilot Scotty Crandlemire in his Cassutt III M, race 12, Outrageous. The unique two-tone purple and silver paint scheme splashed across the wing makes this Cassutt stand out from the many in the field. In 2006, Outrageous was fourth with an average speed of 239.374 mph, which was nearly identical to its fourth-place finish the year before.

Richard Beardsley calls his distinctively decorated blue and yellow Smith Miniplane Rich's Brew. Although the few participating Miniplanes are not competitive against the Pitts and Mong racers, it is a treat to enjoy the variety they provide to the field.

Emitting a buzzing sound like enlarged bumblebees, biplane racers in a line-abreast gaggle come barreling low over the desert, each jockeying for position in the three-dimensional environment of the course.

An overhead view of Stephen Brown's Pitts S-1, Tonopah Low II, shows the comparatively short wingspan of the black and yellow biplane. The Pitts' name is synonymous with aerobatics, for it was Curtis Pitts who spent a lifetime designing and then perfecting what remains a fantastic aerobatic airplane for serious enthusiasts. In the Biplane class, the Pitts aircraft still render great service. In fact, this racer, carrying the unusual race 00, finished third in the 2006 Biplane Gold race with an average speed of 212.237 mph.

In the foreground is a Smith Miniplane, which, ironically, is named Lone Wolf. Sporting race 38, it is flown by Dan O'Marro, a machinist from San Lorenzo, Calif. Like their lightweight counterparts, the aircraft of the Biplane class warrant hangaring during race week as a means of protection from the potentially hostile elements, especially the unforgiving late-day winds. The ambiance in the close quarters of the main hangar, which serves as home during race week to both the Biplanes and Formula One racers, is lighthearted and fun-loving much of the time. There is a cooperative spirit that permeates the atmosphere, a sense that all the pilots and crew members are in the same "boat" and following, quite literally, the same course. In the air they are fierce competitors, but here, in the haven of their temporary home, they are warm and supportive friends.

Negotiating the pylon as closely as possible so as not to lose position, but at the same time guarding against a cut inside the pylon is the trick for the pilots winging their way around the course. This duet of twin-like Formula One racers is closely spaced during the execution of a pylon turn.

Understandably named Rollin', the Pitts S-1S aerobatic biplane raced by airline pilot Robert Vaccariello of Houston, Texas, achieved a fourth-place finish in the 2006 Biplane Silver race with an average speed of 183.061 mph. The red and white starburst paint scheme on the upper wing is an attention-grabber that many Pitts owners have opted to apply.

Resembling a formation jet team or perhaps a squadron on a strafing dive, three L-39s streak across the desert during a Jet class race. Because of the small number of jet competitors, there are not bronze and silver races, but only a gold race. Over the years, course speeds have been clocked in the range of 450 mph for a few of the top performers.

Although L-39s have the reputation of being fuel-efficient, they nevertheless present the airport and air race officials with the requirement of providing a significant quantity of jet fuel on the ramp each race day. In this scene, Phil Fogg's race 8, Ultra Hog, is having its thirst for fuel quenched. Note the military-style camouflage paint scheme as well as the red star on the vertical stabilizer.

Consisting exclusively of the pervasive Aero Vodochody L-39 Albatros jet trainers, the Jet class always provides evenly matched races. Having been produced in large quantities as military trainers for the Warsaw Pact countries during the Cold War, the L-39 type is in plentiful supply. Here, the field of jet competitors lines up in advance of a race. Started in earnest in 2002, the class has had three Gold winners – former astronaut Curt Brown (twice) in race 5, American Spirit, former Unlimited class champion John Penney (twice) in race 2, Pip Squeak, and former T-6 class winner Mary Dilda in race 22, Heartless.

Taxiing his L-39 past the home pylon, Jim O'Neal of Houston, Texas, uses this jet as the pace plane in the Jet class races. It is painted in the motif of the U.S. Navy Blue Angels demonstration aircraft. Of course, this is a fanciful replication since the Blue Angels fly the Boeing F/A-18 Hornet. There is irony in this choice of decoration since the L-39 originated in the former Eastern Bloc-country of Czechoslovakia.

CHAPTER FOUR

THE GALLOPING HERD: COMPETITION AMONG EQUALS

The field of competitors, still bunched together coming out of the chute, tears across the open desert at speeds well in excess of 200 mph. Though the old trainers skim over the desert floor, Reno is a mile high, an altitude at which the aircraft perform commendably.

The clean lines of the airplane's physique marked her as a thoroughbred. When Army and Navy flying cadets first gazed at this engineering marvel of the 1930s and 1940s, they saw an American original, a strong and enduring enchantress, if at times temperamental, that could either fulfill their dream of wings or consign them to the washout list. Attractive yet intimidating, honest but demanding, North American Aviation's AT-6 advanced trainer was known appropriately as the "pilot maker."

Something about the metal monoplane's stately repose gave her the aura of an instant classic, a flying machine so perfectly sculpted and proportioned, it was as if she had always been there ready to tackle the sky. Without the assembly of this archetypal design there would have been a gaping void in aviation. Based on the old adage that if an airplane looks right it will probably fly right, this exquisite, low-wing trainer with the trademark greenhouse canopy fulfilled her promise to turn aspiring aviators into effective fighter and bomber pilots at a time of dire need.

The outbreak of war caused immediate demand for enormous quantities of well-trained airmen, and North American Aviation met the call. The Army Air Corps initiated a design competition in 1937 for what it termed a basic combat trainer. In response, the company reached back to its existing NA-19, a slightly modified version of the NA-16, which was its first airplane. In 1935, the NA-16 was designed and built in less than nine weeks under the tutelage of James "Dutch" Kindelberger, James Leland "Lee" Atwood, and R. H. Rice.

Designated the BT-9 in Army service, the trainer incorporated such modern features as a fully cantilevered, all-metal wing. This model gained favor with the Army and was purchased in meaningful numbers. The Navy also adopted the type and designated it the NJ-1. To satisfy the Army's quest for a new trainer, North American added a more powerful engine to its baseline model, gave it retractable landing gear, provision for armament, and some avionics.

By late 1939, with Europe already mired in conflict, Britain placed a large order for the company's improved trainer with the intent to use them in Canada. There, Royal Air Force student pilots could train without risk of enemy interception. Due to neutrality considerations, the aircraft were flown from North American's Inglewood, Calif., plant to the northern border of the United States, where they were delivered to the RAF by being pushed onto Canadian soil. The

Army Air Corps stepped up its ordering, too, and in 1941 it changed the designation to AT-6.

More than 15,000 of North American's mighty trainers entered service around the world, mainly with U.S. and Commonwealth forces. In the Army Air Force, the advanced trainer's designation was eventually shortened to T-6. The Navy, with its own system for assigning aircraft designators, settled on SNJ. The official U.S. nickname was the Texan. British and Canadian models were called the Harvard. Those manufactured under license in Australia came to be known as the Wirraway. Reflecting the type's universal appeal, various versions were acquired by the air arms of many other countries both during and after the war.

U.S. military cadets started their flight instruction in a primary trainer, most often the estimable Stearman, a two-place, open-cockpit biplane. After mastering the fundamentals of airmanship, cadets progressed to an intermediate or basic trainer, the Vultee BT-13 Valiant (Navy designation SNV-1). This aircraft, nicknamed the "Vibrator," was a bit faster and more complex than the straightforward Stearman. If they made it through the second phase, students were able to get their hands on the two-and-a-half ton Texan.

In this daunting airborne classroom, students had to not only demonstrate their proficiency at flying, but their mastery of complex new systems like the retractable landing gear, the Hamilton-Standard controllable-pitch propeller, and the array of front-cockpit doodads that included a navigational radio for instrument flying.

With a cruise speed at altitude of 170 mph and a maximum speed of more than 200 mph, things tended to happen fast in the Texan. Moreover, with the pistons in the nine cylinders of the 600-horsepower Pratt & Whitney R-1340 hammering away, noise in the cockpit was deafening. You had to know what to do and then do it, which meant being alert, staying ahead of the proverbial power curve, at all times.

Those who could get the hang of it enjoyed flying the brawny aircraft. It is a really good handling aerobatic platform, for it has the requisite power and control responsiveness. However, the real test came in landing the ornery ship. If you were not careful, if you did not respect this idiosyncratic trainer in the context of basic Newtonian physics, then the Texan would sneak up and bite you.

Since the Texan is a tailwheel aircraft, its center of gravity is located aft of the main gear, which in itself makes the ship prone to weathervane when caught in a crosswind on the

The North American Aviation T-6 Texan was a superb platform for imparting the skills required to fly Army and Navy combat aircraft in World War II. It was felt that if you could master the Texan, you could fly anything in the military's inventory. This example on the taxiway is an SNJ-5, a Navy version of the Army's T-6, emblazoned in patriotic colors far removed from the standard military paint schemes of the time. Owned by Jim Good of Casper, Wyo., race 77, Wildcatter competed in the 2006 T-6 Gold race and placed sixth with an average speed of 218.587 mph.

ground. Unlike a tricycle-gear aircraft, which seeks to right itself, the taildragger's wings want to swap ends. The trainer's center of gravity is also high and the inward-folding landing gear legs are closely coupled, adding even more instability.

When three-pointing the big bird, forward visibility is limited from the front seat and nonexistent from the rear seat. Also, at the moment that the tail eases down upon landing, even when the trainer is brought in on its mains, the wing blanks out the tail surfaces, resulting in minimal rudder effectiveness. Clearly, there was plentiful justification for training command's conclusion that its fledgling aviators could fly anything in the inventory if they mastered the Texan.

The challenge inherent in flying the old trainer is part of the lure for devotees like those who bring their T-6, SNJ, or Harvard to participate in the Reno air races each year. There is also the satisfaction that comes from knowing that by keeping a Texan airworthy owners are preserving a very important piece of aviation history. Most of these airplanes were flown by young men destined for combat, bonded by their undying

love of flight and their deep sense of patriotism. The aerial armadas that swept European and Asian skies in defense of liberty were piloted by the Texan's proud progeny.

Some of the two dozen aircraft in the T-6 class are decorated in military markings with varying levels of authenticity. There is *Big Easy*, race number 68, in Marine Corps motif flown by Michael Gillian. Another is the Eberhardt family's *Archimedes*, race 30, which is decked out in the colors of an aircraft based at the old Grosse Ile, Mich., Naval air station. Smack-dab in the middle of their fuselages these ships are emblazoned with the traditional U.S. armed forces red, white, and blue star-and-bars insignia.

After being scavenged from abandoned training fields with crumbled, moss-covered runways that once accommodated an endless stream of loud silvery ships rolling on take-off in rapid succession, these Texans have been brought back to their proper domain of the sky. They now serve as living testimony to a great airplane and the brave hearts who tamed her. For the aged veterans in the grandstands who got their

An intangible, something more than the mere economics of the championship purse, is behind the devotion that is apparent in the pit during race week at Reno. Under a blazing sun far from home, pilots and crews labor on their airplanes. Their work is not glamorous—pulling off cowlings, changing spark plugs, greasing the tail wheel. Invariably, oil drips and the closest sink with running water is a quarter-mile away. For race 5, Big Red, race week maintenance required some diagnostics forward of the firewall. Whatever the problem in 2006, the aircraft managed to do well. Joey Sanders, with a background that includes flying fighters, made it to fifth place in the T-6 Gold race with an average speed of 218.674 mph, edging out Wildcatter.

It is hard to fully convey the extent to which the pilots and crews strive to keep their airplanes looking spotless. The effort is not merely for show or to enhance speed; it is done even more because it is a way of life, a means of validating that everything vital to the ship's operation is in order. Before a race, the crew of race 89, Baby Boomer, gives the racer a complete wipe-down from prop to tail. Fred Telling of Woodcliff Lake, N.J., finished third in the 2002 T-6 Silver race with an average speed of 215.804 mph.

Even champions occasionally have to face unwanted realities. Because air racing involves machinery, there is no way to completely avoid mechanical malfunctions. Highly experienced crop dusting and race pilot Al Goss of Bakersfield, Calif., started having engine problems during a heat at the 2006 air races. He checked and found metal shavings in the oil, which left no choice but to remove the old Pratt & Whitney and send it to the repair shop. A prior T-6 Gold winner, race 75, *Warlock*, sat on the ramp forlornly, canopy covered, absent its engine, spinner, and prop.

first taste of high-performance flying in the front seat of these advanced trainers, one can only imagine the memories kindled by the sights and sounds of such restored beauties.

While the T-6 class pilots are fully aware and appreciative of the type's saga, many have chosen to adorn their airplanes in eclectic schemes with glittering colors. Joey Sanders owns *Big Red*, race 5, which, as the name implies, is a ship that looks as though it has been dipped in catsup, with its nickname splashed across the fuselage in giant white letters. Jim Good's race 77, *Wildcatter*, sports a centered blue band the length of the fuselage accompanied on either side by red stripes, all against a white base coat, with the pattern partially repeated on the wings for an unabashedly patriotic motif.

The vast parking area reserved for the class is a barren sheet of asphalt that takes on a kaleidoscopic look each September with so many boldly painted antique airplanes. Walking through the rows of Texans, neatly arrayed in the pits, is a visual delight. As the pilots and crews tend to their charges, it is not a stretch to imagine this scene resembling the Thanksgiving morning preparations of the one-of-a-kind floats in the annual Macy's parade.

The racing pilots are as varied as the paint schemes on their aircraft. Bud Granley, who flies the perennial T-6 class racer *Lickety Split*, race 9, is a professional air show pilot. Gene McNeely, the pilot of *Undecided II*, race 90, performs regularly with the excellent Aeroshell T-6 precision aerobatic team.

More than a few of the contestants, like past champions Al Goss and Nick Macy, have backgrounds as cropdusting pilots. Some like Wayne Cartwright, who flies *Six Shooter*, race 44, and Michael Gillian, who pilots *Big Easy*, race 68, are business executives. Yet others, like Keith McMann and Mary Dilda, fly for commercial carriers.

If there is a commonality, a shared interest, one would have to say that the flyers who comprise the T-6 class uniformly love their raspy-throated airplanes and the sensual stimulation that comes with opening them up full-throttle at pylon height under the desert's blaring sun. It is as though they are stock car drivers at Talladega, absorbed in their calling. Only here, at Reno, the madcap rush around the course occurs in the three-dimensional realm 50 feet above the ground.

In a scene reminiscent of the halcyon days of massed training flights that were a common occurrence at key instructional facilities like Randolph Army Air Field and Pensacola Naval Air Station, these T-6s cluster at the end of the runway doing their final pre-flight checks—oil pressure, magnetos, flight controls. When they are finally ready, the sky will wake to the raspy sound of propeller blade tips rotating at near-supersonic speed, throwing off an ear-splitting cacophony sure to rattle the bones of any bystander.

When the imposing old trainers pull up in front of the grandstands on takeoff, engines revved to near the maximum manifold pressure setting with prop levers shoved forward into low pitch, the tips of the comparatively short propeller blades twirl at close to supersonic speed, causing a cracking sound as if an inexhaustible supply of wood boards is being fractured one by one at a furious rate. The ear-shattering racket radiates to engulf the hordes of spectators who may momentarily wince, but who revel in the spectacle.

Racing rules require that the T-6 class aircraft remain true to their original design and so, absent major modifications, the racers are much like they were when they rolled off wartime assembly lines. This also means that airplanes in the class are evenly matched. Accordingly, the T-6 heats are guaranteed to result in hair-raisingly close finishes.

When a line of Texans comes rumbling out of the chute, their clamorous racket sounding over the ramp from which they sprang, there is no wild dispersal. Hard as each pilot tries to lurch ahead of the others, the platforms do not possess enough performance variability for one to dramatically over-

take the majority. They are all going as fast as they can but they remain, during that first lap, virtually fixed in relative position to each other as if they are conducting a practice mission from a World War II training base. It is a race of minor refinements to the airframe and of quick wits in the cockpit.

Tricks for eking out an extra few knots include such seemingly insignificant things as sealing an aircraft's seams with tape just before departing the pits, reducing airflow into the notoriously drafty canopy, and tweaking the propeller governor for optimal pitch in level high-speed flight. Arguably, the main determinant in a class where the airplanes are so closely matched is pilot technique. So much depends on knowing your ship and flying it accordingly.

As far back as 1929, famed air racing pilot and aeronautical engineering prodigy Jimmy Dootlittle, then an Army lieutenant, published his *Air Racing Techniques and Tactics*. In this essay, he advised that key to maximizing a racer's performance was to make the turns around the pylons as symmetrically as possible. He warned that pulling too hard would create drag and actually slow the aircraft, whereas turning

The T-6s make their first pass in front of the grandstands after having shot out of the chute upon the air starter's call: "Gentlemen, you have a race!" The desert takes note. The engines' collective gnash reverberates off the ground and every bluff, crag, and ridge in sight. It is the beginning of a wild, adrenaline-pumping ride.

smoothly and evenly would keep airspeed degradation to a minimum. To hasten turns around pylons, he also suggested that the turns be entered a tad high, allowing for a shallow dive during the turn. This sage advice has been handed down mostly by word-of-mouth over the years. To the educated observer, the wisdom gained from the Golden Age of Flight is visibly applied on the Reno course by many of today's participants. The pilots immersed in total concentration, utilizing the knowledge of racing's forefathers like Doolittle and exploiting every maneuvering advantage, are likely to outperform the rest.

In the T-6 class, it is more often cunning and skill than machismo and muscle that decide the outcome. Nevertheless, to the undiscerning eye it appears as if the contestants are impetuously reefing their powerful monoplanes over on their sides in steep banks, consumed in a mad dash with little rhyme or reason except to beat out the other racers in the fre-netic gaggle. Regardless of the prism through which one watches the Texans and Harvards scramble across the open desert, these graceful workhorses of World War II vintage never fail to excite.

During the first half of the 1940s, at airfields dotting the countryside, flying cadets were sweating such details as three-pointing right at the stall speed. Students, obsessed with getting into the air as full-fledged military pilots, could hardly have foreseen then that their beloved "pilot maker" would find an afterlife more than a generation later as a highly coveted antique and as a wildly popular racing platform.

In their own way, the preservationists and the racing pilots sweat the details, too. Like those who flew the Texans and Harvards before them, they strive to attain their lofty goals. As they do so, the spirit of their flying antecedents, the dedicated young men of the World War II generation imbued with dreams of conquering the sky, rides with them.

Coming at you! The batch of T-6s builds speed between pylons. Approaching the course markers, the aircraft must begin transitioning into a bank and turn. The steeper the bank, the heavier the g-load and generally speaking, the greater the drag and the slower the turn. The most successful race pilots make the smoothest turns. It is an art learned and refined over time in the company of peers.

At a distance, it is a majestic sight as T-6s seem to float in a graceful dance around a pylon at staggered heights, yet up close it turns into a frenzied dogfight.

The temperate sky, rugged magenta mountain range, and wispy tumbleweed frame the red-hot racers as they surge across the desert. Of course the pilots are not on sightseeing flights, but instead are concentrating intently on propeller settings and throttle inputs while constantly scanning for other racers.

This is a view similar to that of the pilots in their cockpits as they sprint around the course getting ready to initiate another pylon turn. Leaning into the turn at high speed they begin to feel the weight of the g-forces. Tensing the stomach muscles helps to counteract the ill effects of g-loading.

Jim Good holds Wildcatter *in a near constant radius turn around one of the outer pylons. In 2006, the adroit technique helped him score sixth place in the T-6 Gold.*

Two familiar names at the air races tussle for position. Al Goss and Gene McNeely are nearly neck-and-neck on the T-6 course. Close races happen almost every time because the aircraft, whether the Army T-6 or the Navy SNJ, are so much the same. In the 2002 T-6 Gold race, race 75, Warlock, *finished third with an average speed of 225.361 mph compared to race 90,* Undecided, *which finished fifth with an average speed of 221.189 mph – a mere 4.172 mph difference.*

Gary Miller's race 55, Trophy Hunter, *slugs it out with Wayne Cartwright's race 44,* Six Shooter, *as other Texans are hot on their heels. Miller finished sixth in the 2006 T-6 Silver race with an average speed of 213.621 mph and Cartwright snagged eighth place with an average speed of 211.706 mph. Given the evenness of the match-ups from one airplane to another, these contests frequently see leads established only to fall and then be regained in a never-ending seesaw.*

Looking as if they are locked together, it is an understatement to say that these two T-6s are in a tight race. Wayne Cartwright's race 44, Six Shooter, *and Gene McNeely's race 90,* Undecided II, *could be said to be shooting it out on the course. In 2005, it ended with Cartwright coming in second in the 2005 T-6 Silver race with an average speed of 221.018 mph and McNeely finishing fifth with an average speed of 212.509 mph.*

High-level cirrus clouds somehow manage to cast the T-6 course in a calmer modality. On the outside, Chris Rushing of San Clemente, Calif., leads in race 42, Sugarfoot, while John Zayac of Denver, Colo., follows in race 12, Thumper. In 2005, Rushing took the crown in the T-6 Bronze race with an average speed of 216.676 mph and Zayac scored fourth place in the T-6 Silver race with an average speed of 212.596 mph.

Like a gaudy carousel in the sky, the racers orbit above, their buzzing engine noise substituting for piped music. It is a sight to behold. As the clutch of racers glides past, it is like your favorite horse figure on the merry-go-round twirling out of view. You yearn for it to come back, again and again, so that the thrill never ends.

They just do not build airplanes the way they used to; you'll find no high-tech composites in a T-6. Instead, the fuselage and wings are gleaming metal, the countless rivets shining in the desert light. The T-6 is a symbol of American design ingenuity and production know-how. It trained cadets to be the world's best pilots. Six Shooter *is a beautiful specimen, a T-6G flown by Wayne Cartwright of Salem, Ore.*

In its first career as an advanced military trainer and in its subsequent career as an air racer, the T-6 has retained its reputation as a sturdy workhorse, an honest airplane with a few personality quirks. It will reciprocate good treatment from a competent pilot. Ken Gottschall of Valencia, Calif., chalked up a fourth-place showing in the 2006 T-6 Silver race flying Grace 8 at an average speed of 215.190 mph.

Dennis Buehn's T-6D, race 43, Midnight Miss III, is notable for its striking paint scheme – a two-tone red and white with a partial checkerboard wrapped around the cowling. In 2006 Buehn captured second place in the T-6 Gold race with an average speed of 222.926 mph.

In 2006 Tom Martin of Melissa, Texas, flew race 12, Thumper. That year, Martin came in fifth place in the T-6 Bronze race with an average speed of 203.360 mph.

Longtime race pilot Bud Granley of Bellevue, Wash., pilots race 9, Lickety Split, an SNJ-5. The aircraft has a prominent parking space in the pit and is among the Texans most scrutinized by the spectators. The crew is readily accessible for questions. It seems they are continually tweaking the racer, but somehow always manage to get it in flying condition in time for its scheduled contests. A solid performer in the T-6 Silver races, Granley finished second in 2006 with an average speed of 218.966 mph.

Top Left: It is almost obligatory that the Reno air races would host at least a few candy-apple red T-6s, because the saturated color scheme seems eminently appropriate for the type. This example, race 64, Red Knight, is the Canadian version of the Texan known as the Harvard. As can be seen, it is emblazoned with Commonwealth markings. The aircraft's owner, Keith McMann, is an airline pilot from British Columbia, Canada. McMann is one of the few race pilots from another country to participate in the Reno event. He finished seventh in the 2006 T-6 Silver race with an average speed of 212.876 mph.

Bottom Left: Banking steeply on the backside of a pylon turn, Jim Good in Wildcatter offers a good vantage point of the Texan's overhead planform. The cadets who mastered the T-6/SNJ to receive their silver/gold wings knew the satisfaction of handling an aeronautical gem the likes of which the aviation world has not seen since. The big radial engine, generating the power of 600 horses and clattering reliably, carried the heft of the airframe and enabled core aerobatic maneuvers. The Texan gave innumerable squadrons the pilots needed to win World War II.

CHAPTER FIVE

THE HEAVIES ROAR: *GENTLEMEN, YOU HAVE A RACE!*

Many of the Unlimited class airplanes have been modified, but they all remain familiar, for each is a paradigmatic fighter with an indelible profile immortalized either during or immediately following World War II. These remarkable designs represent the capstone of a disappearing breed—piston-engine combat aircraft. Some lingered in squadrons through the Korean War, but jets were destined for preeminence then and into the future. In time, the old prop jobs were mostly left to rot in the corners of quiet airports or sold off for scrap and then melted down.

Every September since the 1960s, an assemblage of renowned piston fighters, the apex of the lineage, has graced the pits at Reno. During the war, great minds advanced the aeronautical state of the art and emerging industrial behemoths reinvented production modalities. The result was that America pushed piston fighters to near their performance zenith and then manufactured those platforms by the tens of thousands.

Obsolescent Curtiss Tomahawks and Brewster Buffaloes were soon eclipsed by far more capable fighters. In fact some, like the Lockheed Lightnings and North American Mustangs, were so fast that in powered dives they encountered compressibility, the molecular phenomenon associated with flight near Mach one. Although performance in level flight might be boosted for short spurts with customized modifications, these aircraft of the 1940s had taken production piston-powered aircraft technology as far as physics allowed.

The joy of victory manifests itself on the face of John Penney, a three-time Unlimited Gold champion, as he receives the trophy for his impressive win in 2005. Under the wing of race 77, Rare Bear, crew and fans surround Penney, eager to congratulate him. He racked up an average speed of 466.298 mph. In the same year, Penney also entered the Jet class, where he eked out a first-place finish in race 2, Pipsqueak, at an average speed almost as fast as his speed in the Unlimited Gold race. The following year, in 2006, he confined himself to the Jet class, in which he again won first place.

Opposite: The ultimate in air racing is the aptly titled Unlimited class. This grouping of racers is comprised of World War II-era piston-powered fighters. Names like Bearcat, Mustang—seen here, and Sea Fury arouse visions of brimming power, streamlined shapes, polished aluminum, and unbridled speed. These airplanes, the finest and fastest of their day, are the magnet that draws the faithful every September to Nevada's high desert.

At the crack of dawn, the ramp swells with old fighter planes as the sun's soft illuminating rays slip over the horizon. This is Jimmy Leeward's glistening Mustang, race 9, Cloud Dancer.

For Unlimited air racing at Reno, the field is comprised mostly of Mustangs and Sea Furies, with a smattering of Russian-built Yaks, Grumman Bearcats, a Tigercat, even a Wildcat, and a Goodyear Super Corsair as competitors. The world's remaining Kingcobras and Lightnings are in short supply, simply too valuable as collectors' items to race. The key to elevating one's racer into serious contention for the Gold is a major investment in racing refinements. Fighters left in stock condition are at a disadvantage and are unable to match the performance of the heavily modified racers.

The Mustangs and Sea Furies were driven by different design concepts. The Mustang is the earlier aircraft, which started as a North American Aviation project. The British Air Purchasing Commission invested its faith in the company's engineers, who promised to develop a totally new design that would outshine the existing Curtiss P-40. Because Curtiss estimated that it could gear-up for new production of its P-40 within 120 days, the Commission gave North American that long to design, build, and flight test its fighter concept. This was a tall order for any shop, especially North American, because it had never built a fighter. The date was April 24, 1940.

Driven by the imperative of war, the company's design and engineering team produced the prototype's airframe comfortably within the truncated time frame. However, the Allison V-1710 engine was not readily deliverable to this one-off project. When at last the engine arrived in early October, it was installed and ground-tested. On October 26, 1940, the Mustang prototype, designated NA-73X, took off on its maiden flight, which went without any major hitch—a good omen of things to come. A mere 186 days had elapsed since the agreement to proceed. In that time, more than 60,000 man-hours produced 2,800 drawings to transform the Mustang from paper concept to flying machine.

In devising a fighter that would meet the British requirement, North American's designers opted to use a liquid-cooled engine. This meant that the airframe would have a reduced frontal cross-section and thus would encounter less drag. Concerns were raised about the susceptibility of the coolant system to enemy gunfire, but it was theorized that the more aerodynamic configuration would enhance maneuverability that, in turn, would improve the fighter's chances of survival.

The coolant radiator was placed in the lower aft fuselage to minimize drag. Of note, the designers developed an aerodynamic duct system with an adjustable air scoop in the belly to efficiently route airflow for cooling purposes. With this design, additional thrust could be generated by the effect of ram air ejecting the warmed airflow. This had the benefit of counteracting the duct's drag.

The bubble-like canopy of a P-51 provides a prism through which to observe sunrise. September mornings in the high desert are invigorating. The wind is barely discernible, the visibility is a million, and the ceiling is unlimited. Conditions are alluring for those who want to fly. In a few hours the tranquility will be transformed into an unforgettable pageant of brilliant colors and exertive noises emanating from above and lighting a fire within.

In the mid-1930s, ethylene glycol was adopted over water as a coolant for its ability to withstand temperature extremes. With this fluid, less radiator surface area was necessary. Consequently, the Mustang's inlet duct could be tucked up tightly along the lower fuselage, further helping to reduce drag.

Acting on information made available from the National Advisory Committee for Aeronautics, North American chose to use a laminar flow wing for the Mustang. Up until then, no production aircraft had ever employed such an airfoil. Interestingly, the laminar flow wing got some application in 1930's air racing with positive results, and this further persuaded the North American designers to adopt such an airfoil.

The upper and lower sides of a laminar flow wing are symmetrically shaped and they widen steadily from the thin leading edge to a point of maximum camber as far aft chordwise as possible. Such a wing maintains adhesion of the boundary layers of airflow to a point further aft of the leading edge than a normal wing, and this delays the onset of disruptive turbulence at high speeds. Choosing this new type of airfoil held the prospect of a major leap in performance capability.

When the Mustang first entered service, it was not fully achieving its potential. There was one more thing that needed to be done. In early 1942, the assistant air attaché at the American embassy in London recommended that the excellent Rolls-Royce Merlin engine, which had been developed from the "R" engine of the 1931 Schneider Trophy race, be mated to America's new Mustang fighter.

By the autumn of 1942, Mustangs were being flight tested with the Rolls-Royce V-1650 "Merlin" engine. Because Britain was overwhelmed by wartime production needs, the Packard Motor Car Company had actually begun manufacturing Merlin engines under license in Detroit in 1940. Some design and component improvements were made, and the assembly was more automated than the production at Rolls-Royce, where there was a heavy reliance on individual craftsmen. The Packard-built Merlin was rated at 1,380 horsepower on takeoff and up to 1,600 horsepower at the maximum wartime emergency power setting.

Some Mustang modifications, especially to the cooling system, were necessitated by the heavier and more powerful Merlin (as compared to the original Allison). Notably, the new engine required shifting the carburetor air intake from on top of the nose to below it. The tail had to be beefed up as well because the greater performance increased stress on the airframe's aft structure.

This marriage between airframe and powerplant resulted in what was arguably the finest overall fighter of World War II. Fast and maneuverable, the P-51 ruled the skies as America and Britain pressed the air campaign into the heart of Europe. Further refinements, including a bubble-type canopy for improved pilot visibility and external fuel tank fittings for long-range escorts, made it an even more effective fighter. The aircraft was continually upgraded throughout the war and culminated in the lightweight H model. (There was a K model, but this was, in effect, a D model with the troublesome Aeroproducts propeller instead of the reliable Hamilton Standard propeller. Planned L and M models were cancelled at the end of the war.) The model built in greatest numbers and the one with the most impressive combat record was the D model. This is the variant most prevalent at the Reno air races.

Not surprisingly, war surplus Mustangs owned by civilians competed extensively in the postwar Cleveland air races. The P-51s dominated the Bendix cross-country contests. They did not, however, fare as well in the closed-course pylon races where bigger aircraft with air-cooled engines had the advantage.

If Mustangs were to be competitive in pylon racing, they would have to be heavily modified. Interest in drag reduction focused on the "necessary evil" of the cooling system. One of the more unusual ideas showed up on Jacqueline Cochran's P-51, the *Beguine*, which was slated to compete in the 1949 Thompson Trophy race. To eliminate

One of the true stalwarts in the Unlimited class is race 4, Dago Red. The highly modified Mustang has been flown to victory in the Gold races six times and even set the course record in 2003 when pilot Skip Holm punched it up to an average speed of 487.938 mph. That same year, the racer established a new lap record of 512.164 mph. In prior years, pilot Bruce Lockwood tore up the course at the controls of this fantastic machine and also won the Gold. Unfortunately, the awesome racer experienced mechanical problems during the 2006 air races and had to be grounded. Early in race week, a check valve malfunctioned and before the flight was over the engine case started spewing oil profusely. A replacement Merlin was installed in a Herculean effort by Dan Martin's ground crew members, who worked nonstop for 21 hours, but even the substitute engine was flawed. To a large degree, the air races are a test of stamina.

Bob Button's predominantly purple race 5, Voodoo, *is a real standout. However, as race week in 2006 progressed to the final climatic weekend, this highly capable contender fell victim to engine trouble and was confined to its canopied section in the pit. The crew kept working, but the defects were too pronounced for any resolution in the short time remaining before the championship races. Button was disappointed but philosophical, looking to next year to race his formidable P-51 Mustang.*

the aircraft's belly scoop, radiators were placed at the wingtips. This attempt at radical change was short-lived as the racer crashed on the course, killing pilot Bill Odom, and two others on the ground.

The Mustang did return to combat. Within days of the start of the Korean War in June 1950, Mustangs (which had been re-designated as F-51s) were on the scene to provide air cover. However, the air war in Korea was soon to become a conflict between jets. Not really a match for the new Soviet MiG-15, the F-51 was assigned close air support duties.

Another racing type that has become active at Reno also saw service in Korea. The Hawker Sea Fury was developed late during World War II, with the prototype's first flight occurring on February 21, 1945. It was a naval version of the Fury, which had been conceived as a replacement for the Tempest. The first production model, designated F. 10, entered service in August 1947. An improved model, the F.B. 11, began to reach squadrons of the British Fleet Air Arm the following May.

Whereas the Mustang originated early in the 1940s, the Sea Fury was the last of the breed of piston-engine fighter. Hawker engineers incorporated many of the lessons that had been accumulated over the prior six years. Powered by the 2,480-horsepower Bristol Centaurus engine, the published performance of the production fighter was 435 mph at 24,500 feet. The 18-cylinder air-cooled engine used unusual sleeve valves in place of poppet valves. Fundamentally different from the Mustang, the Sea Fury had more heft. Its wing area was 44-square feet larger and it weighed about 1,600-pounds more. Like the philosophy driving Grumman's designs, which included pudgy piston-engine naval fighters such as the Bearcat, Hawker's Sea Fury concept discounted the reduction in frontal cross-section afforded by a liquid-cooled engine. Preference went to the brute power of a big radial engine. It was brawn over finesse.

This divergence between small and large in the approach to racing plane design was characterized in the Thompson Trophy races at Cleveland by Steve Wittman's diminutive

An ongoing practice throughout race week is the testing of engines on the ramp that adjoins the pit. Each Unlimited racer's engine, whether an air-cooled radial or a liquid-cooled inline, is a delicate and finely tuned collection of parts that must run together harmoniously. Here, race 5, Voodoo, undergoes a test run.

configurations on the one hand, and by Roscoe Turner's big-barreled racers on the other hand. In today's Unlimited class races at Reno, the same pattern keeps being replayed with primarily Mustangs on the small end and mostly Sea Furies on the big end. There is no right or wrong. The question as to which of the two types is better comes down to a matter of interpretation.

A feature shared by Mustangs and Sea Furies is their adaptability. Dozens of items were modified in the service life of the Mustang, and when the Reno air races rolled around, many enterprising owners recognized a whole laundry list of tweaks that could be applied to the formidable baseline machine. For one thing, extra cooling during high-speed runs could be accomplished through the installation of spray bars that squirted water onto the radiators. Engine power could be boosted in short, critical spurts through anti-detonation injection (ADI) systems that shoot specially formulated compounds into the engine.

Aerodynamic improvements are the most visible enhancements. These have included fabricating new cockpit canopies. Instead of using the factory's bubble-type canopies, which were designed to provide high visibility for fighter pilots in a combat environment, some owners have installed tiny tapered glass shells, just high enough above the ledge for the pilot to see out, that blend with customized turtledecks for a seamless melding of canopy to fuselage. This type is evident, for example, on Jimmy Leeward's *Cloud Dancer*, race number 9.

Some owners reduce their racers' drag by taking the drastic measure of clipping the wings. Bill "Tiger" Destefani trimmed 30 inches off the wings of his highly modified P-51D *Strega*. Other tricks of the trade include realigning the engine from its slightly nose-high placement so that the thrust line runs along the airplane's longitudinal axis with as little propulsive energy as possible being squandered during a race. Also, the right-of-center position of the vertical stabilizer can be adjusted to neutralize the original design's built-in torque compensation.

Taping over hairline crevices that might exist in some of the metalwork or along the canopy ledge helps to cut down

The blinding paint scheme of race 5, Voodoo, *as seen in the pit in 2002, which was a better year for the souped-up P-51. With Matt Jackson at the controls,* Voodoo *sprinted to third place in the Unlimited Gold with an average speed of 435.614 mph.*

on unwanted drag. Polishing the wing leading edges and other exposed surfaces to a shiny, slippery gloss probably does not do too much to boost performance, but it makes crew members feel that they have stopped at nothing to give their pilot every chance for victory.

Some racers replace the stock engine with a more powerful (and usually heavier) engine. A trio of Mustang owners removed the factory-standard Merlin in favor of the later Rolls-Royce Griffon. Initially conceived as a powerplant for comparatively heavy naval aircraft, the Griffon had a displacement about 36 percent larger than its Merlin predecessor. The newer engine's greater torque caused handling difficulties in single-engine aircraft. The agreed-upon solution was a gear-reduction unit that could accommodate contra-rotating propellers.

Accordingly, racing Mustangs outfitted with Griffon engines have the peculiar-looking twin propellers. Starting in 1975, Roy "Mac" McClain flew a very impressive Griffon-powered Mustang *Red Baron.* This aircraft snared the Unlimited Gold at Reno in subsequent years with Darryl

Greenamyer and Steve Hinton at the controls. Other Mustangs with Griffon engines and the six blades of contra-rotating propellers were the Whittington Brothers' race 38, *World Jet/Precious Metal,* and Gary Levitz's race 38, *Miss Ashley II.*

Sadly, all three came to grief. *Red Baron* was destroyed during the 1979 Unlimited Gold race at Reno, but pilot Steve Hinton survived and has continued to pursue his successful career as a top pilot of exotic aircraft. *World Jet* bellied in at Reno in 1988, but was repaired and began racing again in 1995. Most tragic of all, *Miss Ashley II* suffered a catastrophic structural failure during a high-g pylon turn in a 1999 Unlimited heat, claiming the life of seasoned racing pilot Gary Levitz. In recent times, race 38 has returned to the Reno air races as *Precious Metal.* Ron Buccarelli piloted the ship to a third-place finish in the 2006 Unlimited Silver race with an average speed of 391.366 mph.

Less radical Mustangs have fared better. Notable in recent years have been Tiger Destefani's *Strega* and race 4, *Dago Red,* which has been flown by Bruce Lockwood and Skip Holm. Extensive airframe and powerplant modifications

The ardor to keep the racers sparkling is contagious in the pit. A leisurely stroll up and down the wide aisles reveals that each team dotes on its racing plane, scrubbing the belly there or polishing the spinner here. An especially pristine aircraft at Reno in 2006 was this TF-51D which had been converted from a P-51D. Interestingly, after service in the U.S. Army Air Force and the air forces of Sweden and Nicaragua, an airline captain purchased the fighter and then raced it at Reno in the 1970s as race number 99. After the airline captain passed, Dan Baun bought the Mustang from the estate and engaged a Chino, Calif., restorer to bring the old warbird up to snuff. The restoration and conversion project consumed eight years. In the late summer of 2006, the fighter rolled out of the paint shop wearing the paint scheme and markings (including the Tempus Fugit nose art) of Col. William Daniels, who commanded the 31st Fighter Group in World War II.

are to be found in these racers. An important factor contributing to some of the Mustang successes has been weight reduction.

Starting in 1987, a new racing dynasty began to take shape. That was the first year that *Strega* won the Unlimited Gold, and it represented the beginning of a trend not seen since the late 1960's triumphs of Darryl Greenamyer, when an aircraft became a repeat winner more than twice. *Strega* came back to pick up wins in 1992, 1993, 1995, 1996, and 1997. The five Unlimited Gold races after that were won by *Dago Red*. The course record was established by Skip Holm at the controls of this hot racer in 2003 with an average speed of 487.938 mph.

The designers of the Mustang and the Merlin would certainly be impressed by the performance attained by these highly modified machines. Today's top racing speeds for the old fighters in the Unlimited class represent a leap of about 100 mph from the first postwar Thompson Trophy race in 1946. That is a remarkable advance for airplanes and powerplants that had, as production models, reached their peak levels by the end of World War II. Clearly, the original designs had a profoundly different objective (as well as readiness and durability requirements) than racing requires, but the performance gap between then and now is still significant.

Sea Furies have had their closed-course pylon racing performance improved through replacement of their stock Bristol Centaurus engines with American powerplants—the mammoth Pratt & Whitney R-4360 or the adaptable Wright R-3350. According to engine historian Graham White, the R-4360 Wasp Major was the "masterpiece of air-cooled radial engine design." It has an amazing 28 cylinders in four rows arranged in a helical configuration. The Wasp Major offers 1,560 more cubic inches of displacement and about twice the horsepower of the Vought F4U Corsair's already-successful R-2800 Double Wasp.

The R-4360 was under development during World War II, but quantity production did not start until close to the end of the conflict. It was mated to the Goodyear F2G Super Corsair, a carrier-borne fighter conceived as an answer to the scourge of the Kamikaze. The extra power would enable greater speed, which, in theory, would allow for interceptions at a safer distance from vulnerable aircraft carriers in the Pacific campaign. Although it came too late to enter combat, shortly after the war the Super Corsair proved to be an excellent racing plane.

Known as the Cyclone 18, the Wright R-3350 had a laborious gestation. It was an 18-cylinder, twin-row radial engine manufactured to power the massive Boeing B-29 Superfortress heavy strategic bombers of World War II. Rated at 2,200-horsepower, the early developmental problems were ironed out in time, and the R-3350s proved themselves on the big four-engine bombers. These engines, which roughly approximate the size of the Centaurus, are more amenable to boosting and thus more desirable for racing than the Sea Fury's original powerplant.

Sea Furies proved what they could do when race 8, *Dreadnought*, equipped with a Pratt & Whitney R-4360, captured the 1983 Unlimited Gold with Neil Anderson at the controls. Three years later, Rick Brickert did it again in *Dreadnought*. Thereafter, a Sea Fury did not win the Unlimited Gold until 2006, when Michael Brown zoomed around the course in his race 232, *September Fury*, with an average speed of 481.619 mph. Even though the usual top contenders were nursing mechanical problems, this was the second highest speed in the course's history.

The name of Bill "Rhino" Rheinschild's Hawker Sea Fury, race 117, Bad Attitude, *is not indicative of the mindset anywhere along the flight line at the Reno air races. On its way out of the pit to the ramp and then on to a race, the ship is escorted by crewmembers who ensure that there is wingtip clearance en route. In 2005, Rheinschild took sixth place in the Unlimited Gold race with an average speed of 403.518 mph. The following year he flew about five mph faster but placed seventh, which reflects the generally faster field in the subsequent year.*

Robert "Hoot" Gibson flies race 99, Riff Raff, which is a contender each year in the Unlimited Gold race. Gibson is a former fighter pilot and astronaut who continues to amass an incredible logbook of aeronautical accomplishments. Following his military and NASA careers, he joined an airline and flew passenger jets until having to retire due to the FAA's mandatory age 60 rule for commercial airline pilots. Ironically, he continues to streak across the desert during Unlimited heats in his Hawker Sea Fury. Here, he is holding an impromptu conference on the ramp after a flight in his racer, which can be seen in the background.

Moreover, the next six finishers in the 2006 Unlimited Gold race were Sea Furies, except for Sherman Smoot's race 86, *Czech Mate*, a Yak. *Dreadnought*, with Matt Jackson at the controls, came in second. These results bode well for the future of Sea Furies. One of the lessons seems to be that the heavily modified racers that win the Gold typically retain their title for some time, dominating the class and taking on the mystique of a dynasty. Inevitably, another racer comes along with even more tweaking, which then unseats the reigning champion and the cycle starts over again.

Lyle Shelton's race 77 *Rare Bear*, an unbelievably souped-up Grumman F8F Bearcat, has had nine Unlimited Gold wins starting in 1973 (although the racer had different nicknames on the occasions of its first two wins at Reno in deference to the sponsors at those times). Shelton showed up at the first Reno air racing event in 1964 and has participated on and off ever since. His dynasty rivals that of Darryl Greenamyer, who also had a preference for Bearcats, scoring six of his seven Unlimited Gold victories in aircraft with names like *Conquest 1* and *Smirnoff*.

The Bearcat is the American equivalent of the Hawker Sea Fury in that it was built at the end of World War II as a

naval fighter, capping off a fine lineage of piston-engine fighters, but too late to experience combat in that war. Shelton, a former Naval aviator, decided to give his Bearcat a boost by replacing its factory R-2800 with the bigger R-3350. He also made major modifications to the airframe, including adjustment of the center of gravity so that it is marginally aft. This helps relieve the forces putting downward pressure on the horizontal stabilizer.

With many hours of experience flying high-performance aircraft and his involvement with air racing going back to the 1960s, Shelton developed excellent techniques for skippering his ship in the races. He would often hold his airplane's power in reserve during the qualifying trials and even in the progressive heats, not going full-bore until the Gold contest. At the pylons, he would try not to pile up the g-loading, but take the turns smoothly by starting them early, easing in, and evenly recovering. Eventually, John Penney, a former Air Force pilot, took over flying duties for Shelton and piloted *Rare Bear* to three of its Unlimited Gold victories, in 1994, 2004, and 2005.

From time to time, Unlimited designs have been built entirely from scratch and introduced to racing on Reno's highly competitive course. While promising, both *Tsunami*, which bore a resemblance to Howard Hughes' H-1 racer of the 1930s, and the twin-engine *Pond Racer*, which sprung from Burt Rutan's prolific drafting table, were destroyed in accidents before they could compete in enough races to realize their full potential.

The cost of developing a clean-sheet racer for the Unlimited class is prohibitive and the chances are that the end product will be at best just a smidgen faster than contemporary race winners. The conventional pathway to Unlimited success is to pick a fighter like a Mustang, Sea Fury, or Bearcat, and then reengineer the airframe and powerplant to extract maximum performance during the tortuous few minutes of a pylon race.

The finale of race week occurs in the late afternoon on the last Sunday. If the weather cooperates, the grandstands are packed. The Unlimited racers are towed to the presentation ramp in front of the adoring fans who have waited for this ritual that signifies the impending start of the climactic race.

The hectic pace of activities and the extreme concentration of pilots and crews in their final preparations squelch the inevitable tensions that would otherwise rise to unbearable levels. The world's fastest racing planes are, for this brief interlude, arrayed at show center for all to see.

The World War II-era fighters, aligned perfectly in a neat row, look like exquisitely crafted toys from the upper bleachers, as if an Old World artisan hand-painted each in a distinctive glossy hue. Alas, the airplanes are not toys but real-life machines that, when given the signal, come to life with a blurt, cough, or pop amid an accompanying puff of smoke and the throbbing of paddle-like propellers obediently heaving over from a standstill.

As many as nine powerful racers run-up on the ramp at once, emitting a collective roar that drowns out the announcer's voice and that shakes one's senses. The clattering of thousands of moving parts in dramatically augmented piston engines causes a thumping in the bones. You can almost feel the adrenaline surging as a primeval impulse flitters through the air.

A stray paper cup and some discarded hot dog wrappers are whisked aimlessly into the air behind the cyclonic prop-blast of the mighty aircraft as one by one they taxi from the ramp and past the cheering crowd to the sky that beckons. Watching them peel away for their takeoff and climb-out, the ramp returns to emptiness. The ambiance is transformed briefly into a lull.

Then the calm is pierced as the racers rumble down the runway, starting tortoise-like and then building up

After a race, Riff Raff *is towed back to its parking space in row six of the pit. In the 2006 Unlimited Gold race, Hoot Gibson flew the Sea Fury to a fourth-place finish with an average speed of 437.083 mph.*

One of the most unusual Unlimited racers is race 38, Precious Metal. This highly modified P-51 Mustang is fitted with a Rolls-Royce Griffon engine driving contra-rotating propellers. Owned and piloted by Ron Buccarelli of Hollywood, Fla., this odd-looking aircraft with its six propeller blades, half turning in one direction and the other half turning in the opposite direction, is predicated on the principle of negating the effects of torque. This is the tendency of a prop plane's nose to veer left during high power settings because of the clockwise motion of the propeller, as viewed from the cockpit. In theory, with props turning in opposite directions power is not wasted but channeled into useful thrust. Precious Metal finished in third place in the 2006 Unlimited Silver race with an average speed of 391.366 mph.

steam until, by the time they reach show center, they are already airborne, on their way to form up on the pace plane, a classic Lockheed T-33 flown by former racing pilot Steve Hinton. To help guide the racers, which are taking off in single file, he releases short spurts of white smoke in intervals. West and high, you can see the fighters recede into the distance, discernible shapes shrinking into pencil-point specks and then nothing, just a low-slung sun in the western sky over the open desert, blotting out the lesser objects.

The sagebrush rustles and dust devils eddy. For a few minutes all remains quiet as if this is any other day in the high desert. The dispassion of the Neolithic wilderness belies the thunder about to roll in from the radiant sky.

One of the racers is already in trouble. You could tell something was not right with *Cloud Dancer*. When airplanes are broken, they usually talk to you, and this silvery Mustang, the pride of Jimmy Leeward, had started making strange sounds at takeoff. Cracks in the old fighter's coolant header tank meant disaster was imminent.

Leeward, not knowing exactly what was wrong, but aware that something serious threatened his well-being, let alone his ability to race, declared a mayday and pulled out. He limped back to one of Stead's runways just in time. In flying, especially this kind of flying, the margin between survival and disaster is slim. The declaration of maydays has been a fairly common occurrence in Reno's Unlimited heats, and it is a tribute to the racing pilots that they so often

Unlimited racing is fraught with many potential pitfalls given both the age of the aircraft and the complexity of their systems. None of the racing planes that constitute the field is immune. One of the all-time greats in the class is Lyle Shelton's Grumman F8F-2 Bearcat, race 77, Rare Bear. The massive racer dominated in the late 1980s and early 1990s. In 2004 and 2005, it enjoyed a resurgence, but in 2006 problems with its Wright R-3350 Cyclone engine prevented it from competing. Well-wishers paid their respects at the merchandise table set up to support the stricken racer.

handle the situations with just the right combination of airmanship skills and steely nerves.

To the south, on the closer side of Peavine Mountain, a thin line of white is visible. In another few seconds, a row of dots reveals itself. Stretched line abreast, the racers are formed up on the jet that guides them with a steady hand towards the chute, that invisible channel that serves as unlimited racing's gauntlet.

"Tuck it in, green Sea Fury," the pace pilot intones laconically.

The professionalism honed by years of experience subdues the natural tenseness. The racing pilots are looking sideways at one another's airplanes as if they are in formation school. They have to be neatly aligned before they are released onto the course.

"Yak, pull up a little for me. That's it," the pace pilot gently cajoles.

They keep coming closer to the first pylon. Soon, the crowd can see that these are airplanes; they have a center structure and wings.

"Lookin' good. Keep it lined up. Lookin' good."

It won't be long now. The racers are closing fast; they are almost over the course. The crowd holds its collective breath, and then, over the radio, they hear the staccato, uncharacteristically charged exclamation, "Gentlemen, you have a race!"

Immediately, the jet hauls straight up, clearing the airspace and trailing a vertical plume to give a confirming visual cue that the race has indeed begun. On the way into the high-g pull, the pace plane pilot has been known to sometimes repeat twice more, like the field commander intent on avoiding confusion when issuing the order to commence firing, that "You have a race! You have a race!" His voice tapers off under the crush of the g-load, echoes of the great Bob Hoover resonating in the headsets of all the old-timers on the course.

It is like a strafing run—a line of fighters aiming at the pylon in shallow dives right out of the chute. Still relatively high, they need a little time yet to settle into the left-turning course. They will be much lower when they finish the lap.

Michael Brown's race 232 September Fury *took home the top honors from the 2006 air races. Brown won the 2006 Unlimited Gold race with an average speed of 481.619 mph, which was the second-fastest ever in the sport's 43 years.* September Fury *basks in its moment of glory.*

Strega, a past champion with her wily and aggressive steward Tiger Destefani aboard, breaks ahead of the pack except for one stubborn Sea Fury. The Mustang's red fuselage-white wings whiz past in a surreal blur. Can hunks of aluminum alloy, no matter how wisely shaped and powerfully propelled, really move this fast so low to the ground?

The Mustang's chief rivals, *Rare Bear* and *Dago Red*, did not start because of mechanical problems, a recurring reality for all of the old racing warbirds with their myriad high-performance modifications. For machines that are so robust in the abstract, it is humbling to be reminded of their underlying fragility.

Rounding the pylons at breakneck speed, each pilot jockeys for position, like a NASCAR driver, looking for an opening to make his move—only here it is in three dimensions. Every little push or tug on the control column has spatial and kinetic consequences. One Sea Fury, *Spirit of Texas*, pulls wide to pass another, *Riff Raff*. But it is late afternoon and the already parched desert floor is burning up from the sun's constant heating. You can almost see the thermal waves wafting aloft, roiling the air.

The turbulence is accentuated by the vortices of the racer ahead. The passing airplane is jostled violently, but the pilot presses on. The lead Sea Fury throttles up, and the relative positions of the two do not change. The passing pilot decides to back off and try again on the next lap. Yes, this will all be over in just eight minutes, but that is an eternity up in the sweltering cockpit under the glass canopy with its collateral greenhouse effect. Nor is there any let-up from the deafening noise or the rough-and-tumble ride in the choppy air. Plus, someone is always nibbling at your tail.

Racers fall in line, one after the other, based on their relative speeds. The modifications, the last-minute tweaks, manifest themselves now. It is too late to correct any lingering quirk or gremlin. That will have to wait until next year. For now, all racers are giving it everything they have got.

It looks like *Strega* is making a move on *September Fury*, Michael Brown's gaudily bedecked Sea Fury that has clung to the lead. It is lap five and it is now or never. The Mustang lurches disconcertingly. This is not a good sign. A telltale puff of smoke trails behind the now slowing racer. Suddenly, *Strega* veers off the course and you know that she will not be in

In 2002, race 911, September Pops, *had a dazzling two-tone blue paint scheme. In that year Randy Bailey of Carson City, Nev., piloted the Hawker Sea Fury to fifth place in the Unlimited Silver race with an average speed of 374.187 mph. In 2006, Dan Vance maneuvered the aircraft to an Unlimited Silver win with an average speed of 405.749 mph.*

the hunt any more. The engine problems plaguing the racer all week simply would not let up for the grandest race of all. There is sadness that an old champ misses out on another shot at the title, but the immediate concern is getting her down safely.

"Mayday!" comes the call from Tiger.

Steve Hinton in the pace plane circles above to guide any stricken racers back to the airport. Tiger Destefani has already had his share of maydays during this race week and in prior years, so he nurses his fighter in for a picture-perfect touchdown. Anyone unaware of the emergency in process would think that the man had just made a very nice routine landing.

So powerful, yet so graceful. Dreadnought *spurts across the crystal blue Reno sky on its way to a second-place berth in the 2006 Unlimited Gold race. A prominent veteran of the Reno air races, this hulking old fighter keeps on plugging away. Judging by the angle of bank, pilot Matt Jackson is straining against a considerable g-force. It comes with the territory as the saying goes, and the pilots seem to thrive on it.*

One of the perennial favorites at Reno is race 8, Dreadnought. A two-time Unlimited Gold winner in the 1980s, the Hawker Sea Fury periodically shines at the air races. In 2006, the stalwart captured second place in the Unlimited Gold race with an average speed of 453.559 mph.

Mike Brown keeps pouring it on. His Sea Fury's big Wright R-3350 has been boosted and it shows. Telemetry keeps the racer's crew chief apprized of conditions enabling him to transmit any vital input in real-time as warranted. The airplane sprints in the straightaways and takes the pylon turns very tightly without any visible speed penalty. It is a dual feat of excellent mechanical tinkering and superb pilot technique. Matt Jackson in that marvelous leviathan, *Dreadnought*, pushes to the limit, ADI on and manifold pressure cranked up as high as anyone dare go, but *September Fury* is unbeatable.

The fans get their money's worth for another year. The checkered flag is waved at the home pylon and it becomes official. *September Fury* wins the 2006 Unlimited Gold with the second fastest time in the course's history. It is a goosebump-filled victory for Mike Brown, a first-time Reno champion. In the winner's circle, he wears his tattered straw cowboy hat, pops open a bottle of champagne, and sprays its contents on his crew. He then signs autographs for the hordes of fans who congregate around him after descending from the bleachers.

By now the sun is setting. The wind has finally been tamed. A hint of a chill even materializes on the thinning ramp. The adrenaline has finally come back down. Spectators want to get home or return to their hotels before the darkness sets in.

The airport has opened up again, and the antiques and racers, executive jets and light planes are making hastened departures. Their pilots and passengers also want to reach their destinations before the evening runs too late. This is autumn and the days are beginning their conspicuous compression.

When most of the race fans have dispersed for the parking lots and the ramp is clear, the winning team, all hands present, tows its majestic racer toward

Jimmy Leeward, whose enchanting Leeward Air Ranch in Ocala, Fla., has been developed into a popular pilot community, is one of those habitual Reno contestants in his race 9, Cloud Dancer. Noted for hauling his P-51 around low and close to the pylons, his performances are notable for their drive and energy. Although Cloud Dancer experienced a mechanical problem that caused Leeward to return to the airport before the start of the 2006 Unlimited Gold race, the veteran racer won the Unlimited Bronze race the prior year with an average speed of 343.368 mph.

the sun, back into the pits. It is as though they are chasing the all-too-fleeting glory, hoping to catch and hold onto that last ray of light, seeking to prolong the warmth of their hard-earned triumph. Understandably, they do not want the day to end.

But then this experience really never leaves you. Once you have roamed the pits, joked with crew members and maybe even some of the pilots, you have impressions too vivid and too enriching to ever let go. The camaraderie among men and women of the air knows no equal, and here in the high desert at the crowning point of race week the glue that bonds lovers of flight is in ample supply.

You have seen the world's fastest piston airplanes. Already made famous by pilots and crews of an earlier generation, these fantastic ships now serve another daring cause. They defy the odds and pierce the sky in pursuit of ever-increasing speeds.

The limitless sky, ravishing in its cerulean purity, is the province of infinite possibilities. Strapped into their revivified machines, resolute pilots have taken off, not without risk, intent on striving, reaching, questing. They rose from the roughhewn basin whose surrounding jagged mountain peaks form an undulating horizon. When exhorted to break into furious runs, the racers dashed forward, their occupants abounding in a contagious spirit of expectancy, their hearts full of hope that their aspirations might be achieved.

Wherever you go, the ennobling experience remains a part of you.

Brant Seghetti of Vacaville, Calif., flies race 44, Sparky, which has become one of the most recognizable Mustangs at the Reno air races. In 2005, the aircraft was emblazoned with the logo and colors of the Jelly Belly brand of candies. Corporate branding is likely to continue proliferating among the racers because the sport keeps getting more expensive, and offsets to the rising costs provide welcome relief. The aircraft finished second in the 2006 Unlimited Bronze race with an average speed of 321.467 mph.

This Hawker Sea Fury is decked out in the colors of the Texas state flag and can be thought of as the "lone star" aircraft. Piloted by Stewart Dawson, a retired airline pilot from Celina, Texas, race 105 is called, appropriately enough, Spirit of Texas. Steeply banked, one can easily see the state flag's colors in starburst style. Dawson finished fifth in the 2006 Unlimited Gold race with an average speed of 428.753 mph.

Racing with the number 13 scrawled on the side of your airplane means that you must not be superstitious. The number used to be assigned to the popular Marvin "Lefty" Gardner's Lockheed P-38 Lightning nicknamed White Lightnin'. Now that distinction belongs to this Hawker Sea Fury piloted by Nelson Ezell. In the 2006 Unlimited Gold race, Ezell finished sixth with an average speed of 409.068 mph. A year earlier, he finished fifth with a slightly faster performance.

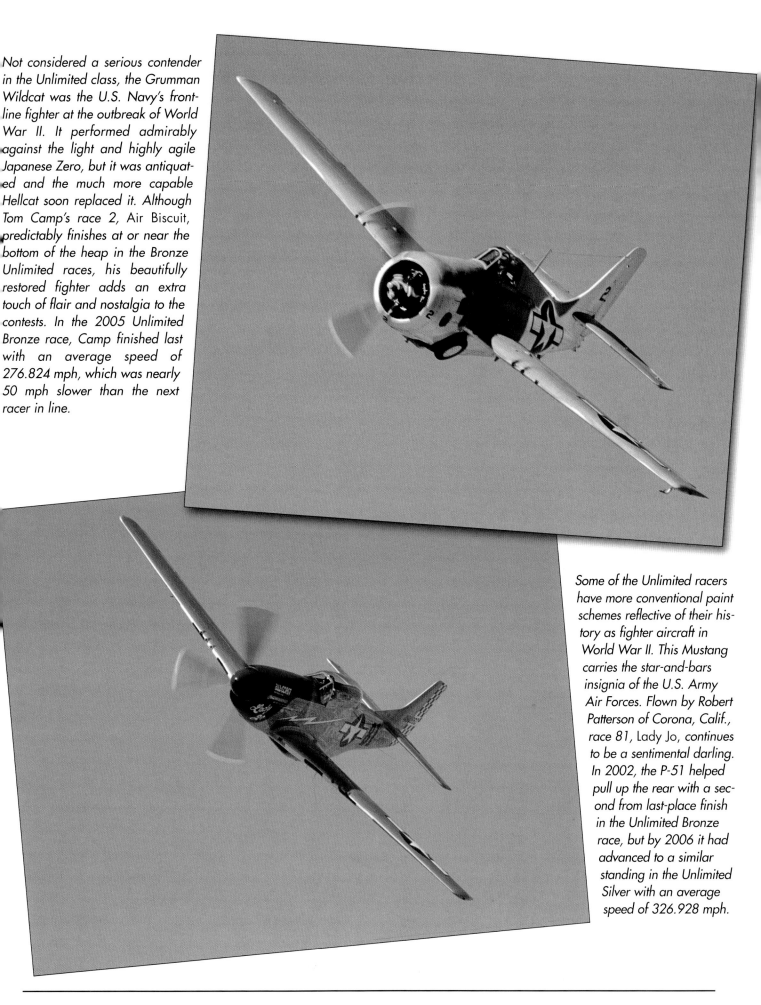

Not considered a serious contender in the Unlimited class, the Grumman Wildcat was the U.S. Navy's front-line fighter at the outbreak of World War II. It performed admirably against the light and highly agile Japanese Zero, but it was antiquated and the much more capable Hellcat soon replaced it. Although Tom Camp's race 2, Air Biscuit, predictably finishes at or near the bottom of the heap in the Bronze Unlimited races, his beautifully restored fighter adds an extra touch of flair and nostalgia to the contests. In the 2005 Unlimited Bronze race, Camp finished last with an average speed of 276.824 mph, which was nearly 50 mph slower than the next racer in line.

Some of the Unlimited racers have more conventional paint schemes reflective of their history as fighter aircraft in World War II. This Mustang carries the star-and-bars insignia of the U.S. Army Air Forces. Flown by Robert Patterson of Corona, Calif., race 81, Lady Jo, continues to be a sentimental darling. In 2002, the P-51 helped pull up the rear with a second from last-place finish in the Unlimited Bronze race, but by 2006 it had advanced to a similar standing in the Unlimited Silver with an average speed of 326.928 mph.

Right: Retired Air Force Lt. Col. "Skip" Holm is the consummate fighter pilot. Awarded three Distinguished Flying Crosses and 25 Air Medals, he received his baptism of fire flying the fast-moving Republic F-105 Thunderchief in Vietnam. Afterward, he became an Air Force test pilot at the Air Force Flight Test Center located at Edwards Air Force Base in southern California. Among the aircraft he has piloted is the Lockheed Martin F-117 Nighthawk, otherwise known as the "Stealth Fighter." In 2002, the first year following the grounding of the air races (and all other civilian flight) because of the terrorist attacks on September 11, 2001, Holm won the Unlimited Gold race in race 4, Dago Red. His average speed that year was 466.834 mph. The following year, he broke the prior record, set in 1990, with a searing average speed of 487.938 mph. Here, Holm has just emerged from his winning racer in 2002.

Two Hawker Sea Furies scramble to stay ahead in an Unlimited heat. The backdrop of clear sky and rugged ridgeline is vintage Reno. By the time the Unlimiteds start racing, the temperature has usually peaked and the air is unsettled. Not infrequently the pilots must deal with naturally occurring turbulence in addition to the demands of the racing itself.

A regular in Unlimited Gold heats is race 99, Riff Raff, expertly handled by former Space Shuttle commander Robert "Hoot" Gibson. The Hawker Sea Fury looks as if it might be doing a knife-edge pass in an air show act, but a tight turn in a hotly contested air race is the reason for this bank of nearly 90 degrees . The stresses at such moments are onerous for both airframe and pilot. It requires enormous commitment to be an air-racing pilot.

A triumphant finish in the Unlimited Gold race is cause for celebration. Sharing the joy of his sweet victory in 2002, Skip Holm and some family members greet well-wishers on the starboard wing of Dago Red.

Posing for pictures by September Fury, Michael Brown and his family and crew are all smiles. It is always an arduous path to the winners' circle and a thrill for those lucky enough to occupy it.

The sun sinks below the western mountains, the spectators vacate the ramp, and soon it is time for the pilot, his family, and team-mates to put the faithful racer back in its designated parking spot for the evening. It has been a long but rewarding day, and the entire Dago Red team arrays itself on the wing facing the setting sun for the tow back to their place in the pit—a fitting conclusion to a wondrous week at the Reno air races.

The winners' circle can become rather festive in the immediate aftermath of the Unlimited Gold race, the ultimate race in the week-long flying at Reno. In 2006, Michael Brown of Carson City, Nev., flew race 232, September Fury, to victory with a near-record average race speed of 481.619 mph.

One of Michael Brown's teammates proudly raises the Unlimited Gold trophy in front of the 2006 champion racer, September Fury. For more than four decades the fastest piston aircraft and pilots have graced this tarmac. The tradition is expected to continue for many years to come.

CHAPTER SIX

PAINTED NOSES: ARTWORK OF THE AIR RACERS

The fastest Unlimited class racer at Reno in 2006 was Michael Brown's September Fury, a Hawker Sea Fury that features the same underlying nose art design as his other Sea Fury.

It would be hard to imagine the rows of racing airplanes at Reno without their nose art. The pithy renderings, provocative statements, patriotic depictions, historic emblems, and personal symbols etched onto the noses of the racers provides a distinguishing identity, an unambiguous expression of the owner's or pilot's character and outlook.

Of course, nose art is most commonly associated with World War II military aircraft. In the early 1940s, tens of thousands of planes were churned out of American factories. Applying mass production techniques of the auto industry to airplane manufacturing, the Ford Motor Company's Willow Run assembly plant in Ypsilanti, Michigan, for example, produced a B-24 heavy bomber every hour.

Many of the aircraft were christened by their pilots at the front. Some of the sobriquets resonated powerfully then and continue to even now. *Memphis Belle* was the nickname of a B-17 that came to symbolize the fighting spirit and staying power of America's Eighth Air Force in the air war over Europe. The names *Marge* and *Glennis* inscribed across the noses of a P-38 and P-51, respectively, signified the affection of fighter aces for their sweethearts and the yearning to be back home with them. *Enola Gay* conjured up a whole range of emotions, for the B-29 emblazoned with this moniker was the first of two Superfortresses to drop atomic bombs in anger.

In most cases the artwork was not pictorially memorable or technically gifted. Often a crew chief with an artistic bent would be called upon to re-create the vision of his pilot on an olive drab or bare aluminum surface. The desired paints were not always available, and if so the image took shape without the requisite hues. Regardless, the point that the pilot sought to convey with his nose art—death to Hitler, attachment to the hometown gal, admiration for a family elder, etc.—came to be understood by those who mattered most, the pilot's squadron mates.

A few of the novice illustrators proved to have the professional's touch, and their artistic creations on the sides of combat flying machines prompted the art world to eventually take notice. Sublime representations of voluptuous women in risqué poses embellished the outward appearance of some bombers and fighters, and these striking portrayals of pin-up girls turned into a part of cultural history.

Sexual suggestiveness in the artwork was rampant and by today's standards far too overt for military aircraft. Part fantasy, part escapist, part machismo, these renderings became integral to the way in which the war's aircraft have been remembered by succeeding generations. By contrast, the military's current low-visibility paint schemes and delicate radar-eluding materials do not often allow for application of customary nose art. In any event, reflecting society's prevailing attitudes, sexually explicit depictions are prohibited on today's U.S. military aircraft, some of whose pilots and flight crew members are women.

When it comes to the Reno air races, the decoration of the whole airplane, not just the area around the cowling, is a matter of personal choice. Owners paint their ships any way they want. The resulting paint schemes, wherein the nose art is just an accent on the cake's icing, bring a remarkable visual vibrancy to the ramp and make glorious conversation pieces.

Of course, some owners opt to keep their racers in quasi-authentic markings with only the mandatory race number disturbing the aesthetic. More often, the racers appear in eye-popping colors—a psychedelic starburst or a candy-apple red or a yellow-and-orange two-tone. *September Fury*, which features a red-and-yellow scheme, has a stylized white-hot exhaust trailing from the vicinity of the engine's exhaust stacks. Then there is *Voodoo* with its delightfully garish purple gloss highlighted by black-and-yellow elements. Not to be outdone, *Dago Red* is a moving art show. It is drenched in a blinding vermilion with wavy bands of white puffs mixed with a consistent lemon yellow spanning the length of the fuselage, like a visualization of thrust blowing from nose to tail.

It is an understatement to say that the nose art on the Reno racers is eclectic. Some of the painted-on nicknames evoke a particular personality, perhaps none more so than *Ole Yeller*, the egg-yolk P-51 that was piloted for years by Bob Hoover. Hoover's place at Reno is firmly established; in addition to having performed in the flying displays with regularity, he served for a long time as the official pace pilot and starter for the Unlimited races. From the perch of his Mustang, he would sententiously snap his trademark phrase for commencing the contests—"Gentlemen, you have a race!"

Although in recent years John Bagley of Rexburg, Idaho, has raced *Ole Yeller*, it is inextricably linked to that aging airman who first flew the type in the Army Air Force, who went to work for the company that had built it, and who immortalized it at the air races over the Nevada desert. None of the old-timers at Reno can look at the wonderful old fighter without memories of the great Bob Hoover coming to mind. The distinctively decorated Mustang will be remembered as Hoover's airplane for as long as it retains the austere scheme

Indicative of the plays on words and the double meanings of some of the clever nicknames painted on the noses of the Reno air racers is this appellation, Ms. Take, appearing on a T-6.

and recognizable nickname from when the famous airman used it to stamp his imprint in the sky.

Some nicknames have been predictable, like Darryl Greenamyer's winning Unlimited racer in 1969 and 1971, *Conquest 1*. While aircraft in the Sport class are typically not as decorative as in the heavier classes, Scott Germain's Lancair is called *Unleashed*, another foreseeable appellation. Up the same alley is Gary Miller's SNJ-3 (T-6) that goes by the title *Trophy Hunter*.

Stewart Dawson's Hawker Sea Fury *Spirit of Texas*, as one might expect, wears the Texas flag over the fuselage and wings. *Merlin's Magic* is a P-51 that races with a Merlin engine. The nose art includes Mickey Mouse in a magician's outfit waving a wand next to the words that are painted directly beneath the exhaust stacks. One of the T-6 racers goes by the nickname *Six Shooter*.

Artwork is sometimes applied for straightforward commercial reasons. Past championship holder *Rare Bear* prominently features the logo and colors of Aeroshell, the oil company's aviation brand. The P-51 *Sparky* was left substantially free of decoration until the Jelly Belly candy company decided to use the air races as a promotional venue. Then, *Sparky* appeared as a flying advertisement for the branded jelly beans with oversize renderings of the company's products emblazoned all over the fuselage and wings. Bob Odegaard's historical replication of the artwork on his magnificently restored Super Corsair showcases the sponsorship from the late 1940s of Standard Oil of Ohio, known as Sohio.

Great artwork combines beautiful paint jobs with poignant messages. The silvery Mustang with the sash-like crimson accent from the tip of the spinner to halfway back over the cowl projects a solidity and grace. Neat calligraphy spells out the nickname *Miracle Maker*. Through its yearly appearance at Reno, the airplane broadcasts the message contained in its nose art. That spare epistle speaks volumes about the dreams embodied in the soul of air racing. Could it be telling us that our conviction accompanied by concerted effort actually allows us to make miracles happen?

Another Unlimited aroused such a sentiment some years back. First, the gorgeous airplane, by the sheer force of its rarity among versions of the type and the singularity of its motif, grabbed your attention. She was one of those exceptional early model P-51 Mustangs. Painted a pure cherry red like an old fire engine, this unique racer was not that fast, but what a sight it was. Wearing its sobriquet proudly in a shaded script along the nose, you could see the golden lettering stand out from afar against the uniform base coat. They called her *The Believer*. You could read your own meaning into the audacious title. It was unquestionably subject to interpretation. Among the myriad possibilities, perhaps one might reasonably conclude that in its simple wording it meant to convey the idea that if you believe then by believing, as you apply all your humanly powers, your dreams just may come true. What an admirable and heartwarming intimation.

The nose art decorating the SNJ-4 Sugarfoot includes a bear with an apparently sugarcoated foot.

Dennis Buehn's Midnight Miss III is a stunning red-and-white T-6D with checkerboard accents.

The nose art on SNJ-3 Trophy Hunter *contains a depiction of the crosshairs of a gun sight.*

The words Hot Off The Press *appear with a flaming background on race 21, an SNJ-5 flown by Rick Siegfried of Downers Grove, Ill.*

Miss Universe is inscribed on race 1, a T-6D belonging to Jason Somes of Simi Valley, Calif. Note the open inspection cover.

Riff Raff is the unlikely nickname on the nose of the Hawker Sea Fury piloted by highly respected former fighter pilot and astronaut Robert "Hoot" Gibson of Murfreesboro, Tenn.

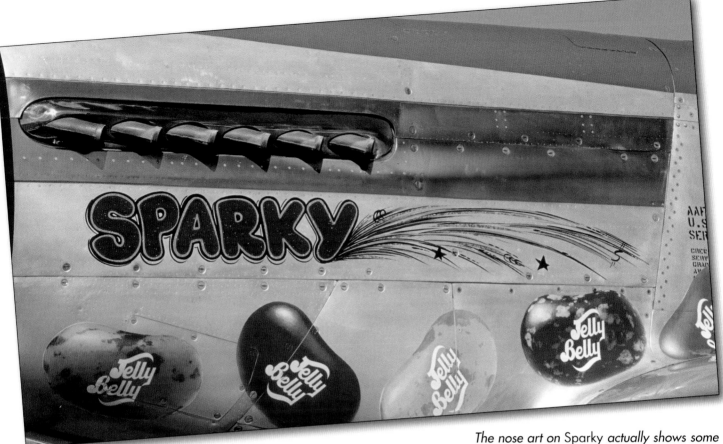

The nose art on Sparky actually shows some sparks flying. Also, there is an extensive application of oversize renderings of Jelly Belly candies reflecting the corporate sponsorship of Brant Seghetti's P-51 Mustang.

As one might expect, the nose art on Jimmy Leeward's P-51 Cloud Dancer promotes the owner's real estate development in Ocala, Fla., the lovely Leeward Air Ranch.

Kind of bland for nose art, but perhaps reflective of the theme is this straightforward nickname, Bad Attitude, *painted on race 117, the Hawker Sea Fury raced by Bill Rheinschild of Van Nuys, Calif.*

This rare P-51A, one of the initial production models of the superb Mustang, is owned by Gerry Gabe and flown by longtime air racing pilot Dave Morss of Redwood City, Calif. The fighter, restored to the motif of the era in which it was first operated, carries the nickname Polar Bear, *with concomitant artwork.*

The Griffon-powered Precious Metal *has kept decoration to a minimum, but note the cans, connected by a chain, that serve as caps for each exhaust stack. Now that is improvisation.*

This North American P-51 Mustang Unlimited racer, owned by Dan Martin of San Jose, Calif., remains true to the type's World War II background. Ridge Runner III *shows 20 victory markings.*

A rare Grumman F7F Tigercat, part of Michael Brown's stable of racing aircraft, is emblazoned with this nose art depicting a cartoon Big Bossman.

Michael Brown's Hawker Sea Fury, September Pops, has been decorated with artwork showing a couple of storks delivering bombs wrapped in diapers. The nose art is taken from a World War II Liberator bomber whose pilots both had expectant wives during the war.

AIR RACING OVER RENO

Pipsqueak *was the winning L-39 in 2005 and 2006, piloted by John Penney. With average speeds of 454.194 mph and 470.195 mph, the nickname hardly seems appropriate.*

Top Left: By any measure, Stead Fast *is a fitting nickname for an air racing aircraft. The first word is an obvious reference to Bill Stead, the founder of the Reno air races and to the airport where the air races take place. The second word clearly highlights the notion of speed. Taken together, the words represent a quality required for winning on the course. Will Whiteside of Windsor, Calif., owns and flies this Yak 3U.*

Bottom Left: Technically not nose art but wingtip tank art, Giant Killer *is the nickname of the bright red L-39 piloted by Cliff Magee of Tulsa, Okla.*

APPENDIX I

WINNING RACERS AT THE NATIONAL CHAMPIONSHIP AIR RACES, RENO, NEVADA, 1964-2006

Unlimited Class

Year	Pilot	Race number, name	Speed (mph)
1964	Mira Slovak	80 *Miss Smirnoff*	376.84
1965	Darryl Greenamyer	1 *Greenamyer Bearcat*	375.10
1966	Darryl Greenamyer	1 *Smirnoff*	396.22
1967	Darryl Greenamyer	1 *Smirnoff*	392.62
1968	Darryl Greenamyer	1 *Greenamyer Bearcat*	388.65
1969	Darryl Greenamyer	1 *Conquest 1*	412.63
1970	Clay Lacy	64 *Miss Van Nuys*	387.34
1971	Darryl Greenamyer	1 *Conquest 1*	413.99
1972	Gunther Balz	5 *Roto-Finish Special*	416.16
1973	Lyle Shelton	77 *7¼% Special*	428.16
1974	Ken Burnstine	33 *Miss Suzie Q*	381.48
1975	Lyle Shelton	77 *Aircraft Cylinder Special*	429.92
1976	Marvin "Lefty" Gardner	25 *Thunderbird*	379.61
1977	Darryl Greenamyer	5 *Red Baron*	430.70
1978	Steve Hinton	5 *Red Baron*	415.46
1979	John Cocker	6 *Sumthin' Else*	422.30
1980	Mac McClain	69 *Jeannie*	433.01
1981	Skip Holm	69 *Jeannie*	431.29
1982	Ron Helve	4 *Dago Red*	405.09
1983	Neil Anderson	8 *Dreadnought*	425.24
1984	Skip Holm	84 *Stiletto*	437.621
1985	Steve Hinton	1 *Super Corsair*	438.186
1986	Rick Brickert	8 *Dreadnought*	434.488

Year	Pilot	Race number, name	Speed (mph)
1987	Bill "Tiger" Destefani	7 *Strega*	452.559
1988	Lyle Shelton	77 *Rare Bear*	456.821
1989	Lyle Shelton	77 *Rare Bear*	450.910
1990	Lyle Shelton	77 *Rare Bear*	468.620
1991	Lyle Shelton	77 *Rare Bear*	481.618
1992	Bill "Tiger" Destefani	7 *Strega*	450.835
1993	Bill "Tiger" Destefani	7 *Strega*	455.380
1994	John Penney	77 *Rare Bear*	424.407 (Super Gold)
1995	Bill "Tiger" Destefani	7 *Strega*	469.029
1996	Bill "Tiger" Destefani	7 *Strega*	469.948
1997	Bill "Tiger" Destefani	7 *Strega*	453.130
1998	Bruce Lockwood	4 *Dago Red*	450.599
1999	Bruce Lockwood	4 *Dago Red*	472.332
2000	Skip Holm	4 *Dago Red*	462.007
2001	[No races due to the 9/11/2001 terrorist attacks, which grounded all aircraft]		
2002	Skip Holm	4 *Dago Red*	466.834
2003	Skip Holm	4 *Dago Red*	487.938
2004	John Penney	77 *Rare Bear*	469.961
2005	John Penney	77 *Rare Bear*	466.298
2006	Michael Brown	232 *September Fury*	481.619

T-6 Class

Year	Pilot	Race number, name	Speed (mph)
1968	Hendrick Otzen	1 *Condor*	181.32
1969	Ben Hall	7 *Miss Meridian Favors*	190.90
1970	[No T-6 class races in 1970]		
1971	Bob Mitchem	94 *Miss Colorado*	205.85
1972	Mac McClain	25 *Miss Eufaula*	201.59
1973	Bill Turnbull	72 *Old Ironsides*	206.60
1974	Pat Palmer	99 *Gotcha*	211.35
1975	Pat Palmer	99 *Gotcha*	207.19
1976	Pat Palmer	99 *Gotcha*	210.68
1977	Ralph Twombly	41 *Spooled Up*	209.66
1978	Ralph Rina	73 *Miss Everything*	205.71
1979	[No T-6 class races in 1979]		
1980	[No T-6 class races in 1980]		
1981	John Mosby	44 *Miss Behavin'*	222.78
1982	Ralph Twombly	44 *Miss Behavin'*	214.90
1983	Richard Sykes	14 *The Mystery Ship*	225.94
1984	Ralph Rina	73 *Miss Everything*	217.26

Year	Pilot	Race number, name	Speed (mph)
1985	Randi Difani	18 *Thunderbolt*	213.89
1986	Eddie Van Fossen	27 *Miss TNT*	223.450
1987	Eddie Van Fossen	27 *Miss TNT*	226.362
1988	Eddie Van Fossen	27 *Miss TNT*	229.264
1989	Tom Dwelle	7 *Tinker Toy*	222.326
1990	Tom Dwelle	7 *Tinker Toy*	229.264
1991	Eddie Van Fossen	27 *Miss TNT*	227.028
1992	Eddie Van Fossen	27 *Miss TNT*	234.766
1993	Eddie Van Fossen	27 *Miss TNT*	226.885
1994	Eddie Van Fossen	27 *Miss TNT*	224.704
1995	Charles Hutchins	21 *Mystical Power*	231.430
1996	Sherman Smoot	86 *Bad Company*	221.677
1997	Mary Dilda	21 *Mystical Power*	228.003
1998	Jack Frost	47 *Frostbite*	229.254
1999	Nick Macy	6 *Six Cat*	229.396
2000	Nick Macy	6 *Six Cat*	228.299
2001	[No races due to the 9/11/2001 terrorist attacks, which grounded all aircraft]		
2002	Tom Campau	21 *Mystical Power*	231.614
2003	Nick Macy	6 *Six Cat*	235.264
2004	Al Goss	75 *Warlock*	238.079
2005	Mary Dilda	22 *Two of Hearts*	237.180
2006	Nick Macy	6 *Six Cat*	235.609

Formula One Class

Year	Pilot	Race number, name	Speed (mph)
1964	Bob Porter	14 *Little Gem*	193.44
1965	Bob Porter	39 *Deerfly*	202.14
1966	Bill Flack	92 *Rivets*	193.10
1967	Bill Flack	92 *Rivets*	202.70
1968	Ray Cote	16 *Shoestring*	214.61
1969	Ray Cote	16 *Shoestring*	225.55
1970	Ray Cote	16 *Shoestring*	220.07
1971	Ray Cote	16 *Shoestring*	224.14
1972	Ray Cote	16 *Shoestring*	223.95
1973	Ray Cote	16 *Shoestring*	231.26
1974	Ray Cote	16 *Shoestring*	235.42
1975	Ray Cote	16 *Shoestring*	227.46
1976	Vince Deluca	71 *Lil' Quickie*	228.75
1977	John Parker	93 *Top Turkey*	226.12
1978	[No Formula One class championship race due to weather]		
1979	John Parker	3 *Wild Turkey*	240.09
1980	John Parker	3 *American Special*	249.07
1981	Ray Cote	16 *Shoestring*	232.13
1982	Jon Sharp	43 *Aero Magic*	224.52
1983	Chuck Wentworth	69 *Flexi-Flyer*	239.02
1984	Ray Cote	44 *Judy*	236.068
1985	Ray Cote	44 *Judy*	229.09
1986	Jon Sharp	43 *Aero Magic*	239.614

Year	Pilot	Race number, name	Speed (mph)
1987	Alan Preston	44 *Sitting Duck*	232.989
1988	Alan Preston	44 *Sitting Duck*	240.748
1989	Ray Cote	4 *Alley Cat*	231.251
1990	James Miller	14 *Pushy Cat*	237.405
1991	Jon Sharp	3 *Nemesis*	245.264
1992	Jon Sharp	3 *Nemesis*	238.175
1993	Jon Sharp	3 *Nemesis*	246.849
1994	Jon Sharp	3 *Nemesis*	248.911
1995	Jon Sharp	3 *Nemesis*	249.904
1996	Jon Sharp	3 *Nemesis*	238.950
1997	Jon Sharp	3 *Nemesis*	245.043
1998	Jon Sharp	3 *Nemesis*	245.257
1999	Jon Sharp	3 *Nemesis*	243.513
2000	Ray Cote	4 *Alley Cat*	245.912
2001	[No races due to the 9/11/2001 terrorist attacks, which grounded all aircraft]		
2002	Gary Hubler	95 *Mariah*	249.560
2003	Gary Hubler	95 *Mariah*	253.823
2004	Gary Hubler	95 *Mariah*	250.108
2005	Gary Hubler	95 *Mariah*	252.302
2006	Gary Hubler	95 *Mariah*	257.047

Biplane Class

Year	Pilot	Race number, name	Speed (mph)
1964	Clyde Parsons	11 *Parsons Twister*	144.57
1965	Bill Boland	3 *Boland Mong*	148.68
1966	Chuck Wickliffe	11 *Clark Dollar Special*	147.72
1967	Bill Boland	3 *Boland Mong*	151.64
1968	Dallas Christian	99 *Mongster*	175.13
1969	Dallas Christian	99 *Mongster*	184.02
1970	Bill Boland	3 *Boland Mong*	177.45
1971	Bill Boland	3 *Prop Wash*	181.67
1972	Don Beck	89 *Sorceress*	189.72
1973	Sid White	1 *Sundancer*	194.95
1974	Sid White	1 *Sundancer*	198.17
1975	Don Beck	89 *Sorceress*	198.99
1976	Don Beck	89 *Sorceress*	202.15
1977, 1978, 1979	[No Biplane class races in 1977, 1978, 1979]		
1980	Pat Hines	1 *Sundancer*	206.62
1981	Pat Hines	1 *Sundancer*	209.44
1982	Don Fairbanks	5 *White Knight*	172.73 [Sport Div.]
1982	Pat Hines	1 *Sundancer*	209.40 [Racing Div.]
1983	Don Fairbanks	5 *White Knight*	179.59 [Sport Div.]
1983	Pat Hines	1 *Sundancer*	217.60 [Racing Div.]

Year	Pilot	Race number, name	Speed (mph)
1984	Don Beck	00 *Miss Lake Tahoe*	189.97
1985	Don Beck	00 *Miss Lake Tahoe*	195.62
1986	Alan Preston	00 *Miss Lake Tahoe*	192.665
1987	Tom Aberle	31 *Long Gone Mong*	196.473
1988	Alan Preston	00 *Top Cat*	205.918
1989	Tom Aberle	40 *Wanna Play II*	196.140
1990	Danny Mortensen	91 *Amsoil Pacific Flyer*	192.278
1991	Takehisa "Ken" Ueno	18 *Samurai*	195.273
1992	Jim Smith, Jr.	88 *Glass Slipper*	193.893
1993	Patti Johnson-Nelson	40 *Full Tilt Boogie*	208.466
1994	Earl Allen	21 *Class Action*	203.311
1995	Patti Johnson-Nelson	40 *Full Tilt Boogie*	202.124
1996	Patti Johnson-Nelson	40 *Full Tilt Boogie*	212.811
1997	Earl Allen	21 *Class Action*	198.736
1998	Jim Smith, Jr.	88 *Glass Slipper*	201.599
1999	Dave Rose	3 *Rags*	210.122
2000	Dave Rose	3 *Rags*	209.434
2001	[No races due to the 9/11/2001 terrorist attacks, which grounded all aircraft]		
2002	Dave Rose	3 *Rags*	224.200
2003	Dave Rose	3 *Frightful*	219.181
2004	Tom Aberle	62 *Phantom*	237.932
2005	Andrew Buehler	62 *Phantom*	230.827
2006	Tom Aberle	62 *Phantom*	251.958

Sport Class

Year	Pilot	Race number, name	Speed (mph)
1998	David Morss	99 Lancair IV	308.184
1999	David Morss	99 Prototype	319.671
2000	David Morss	99 Lancair IV	328.045
2001	[No races due to the 9/11/2001 terrorist attacks, which grounded all aircraft]		
2002	Darryl Greenamyer	33 Lancair Legacy	328.967
2003	Darryl Greenamyer	33 Lancair Legacy	324.497
2004	Darryl Greenamyer	33 Lancair Legacy	333.876
2005	Darryl Greenamyer	33 Lancair Legacy	364.950
2006	Jon Sharp	3X *Nemesis NXT*	360.389

Jet Class

Year	Pilot	Race number, name	Speed (mph)
2000	Jimmy Leeward	Jet Demo	No recorded time.
2001	[No Jet class demo or Jet class race]		
2002	Curt Brown	5 *American Spirit*	456.540
2003	Mary Dilda	22 *Heartless*	434.019
2004	Curt Brown	5 *American Spirit*	439.707
2005	John Penney	2 *Pip Squeak*	454.194
2006	John Penney	2 *Pip Squeak*	470.195

APPENDIX II

FURTHER READING

Allard, Noel. *Speed: The Biography of Charles W. Holman.* Eagan, Minnesota: Flying Books, 1986.

Berliner, Don. *Victory Over the Wind: A History of the Absolute World Air Speed Record.* New York: Van Nostrand Reinhold Company, 1983.

——. *The Complete Worldwide Directory of Racing Airplanes, Volume 1.* Destin, Florida: Aviation Publishing, Inc., 1997.

——. *Unlimited Air Racers.* Osceola, Wisconsin: Motorbooks International, 1992.

Bingham, Victor F. *Merlin Power: The Growl Behind Air Power in World War II.* Shrewsbury, England: Airlife Publishing Ltd., 1998.

Bohrer, Walt. *Black Cats and Outside Loops: Tex Rankin, Aerobatic Ace.* Oregon City, Oregon: Plere Publishers, Inc., 1989.

Davisson, Budd. *Pitts Specials: Curtis Pitts and His Legendary Biplanes.* Osceola, Wisconsin: Motorbooks International, 1991.

Dwiggins, Don. *They Flew the Bendix Race: The History of the Competition for the Bendix Trophy.* Philadelphia: J. B. Lippincott Co., 1965.

Gandt, Robert. *Fly Low, Fly Fast: Inside the Reno Air Races.* New York: Viking Books, 1999.

Glines, Carroll V. *Roscoe Turner: Aviation's Master Showman.* Washington, D.C.: Smithsonian Institution Press, 1995.

Grantham, A. Kevin and Nicholas A. Veronico. *Griffon-Powered Mustangs, Raceplane Tech Series, Volume 1.* North Branch, Minnesota: Specialty Press, 2000.

Gwynn-Jones, Terry. *The Air Racers: Aviation's Golden Era 1909-1936.* London: Pelham Books Ltd., 1984.

Handleman, Philip. *Speedsters: Today's Air Racers in Action.* Osceola, Wisconsin: Motorbooks International, 1997.

——. *Air Racing Today: The Heavy Iron at Reno.* Osceola, Wisconsin: MBI Publishing Co., 2001.

Hoover, R. A. "Bob" with Mark Shaw. *Forever Flying: Fifty Years of High-Flying Adventures, From Barnstorming in Prop Planes to Dogfighting Germans to Testing Supersonic Jets.* New York: Pocket Books, 1996.

Hull, Robert. *September Champions: The Story of America's Air Racing Pioneers.* Harrisburg, Pennsylvania: Stackpole Books, 1979.

——. *A Season of Eagles.* Bay Village, Ohio: Bob Hull Books, 1984

Jerram, Mike. *Reno 2: The National Championship Air Races*. London: Osprey Publishing Limited, 1986.

Kinert, Reed. *American Racing Planes and Historic Air Races*. Chicago: Wilcox and Follett Co., 1952.

———. *Racing Planes and Air Races: A Complete History, Volume I, 1909-1923*. Fallbrook, California: Aero Publishers, 1969.

———. *Racing Planes and Air Races: A Complete History, Volume II, 1924-1931*. Fallbrook, California: Aero Publishers, 1969.

———. *Racing Planes and Air Races: A Complete History, Volume III, 1932-1939*. Fallbrook, California: Aero Publishers, 1969.

———. *Racing Planes and Air Races: A Complete History, Volume IV, 1946-1967*. Fallbrook, California: Aero Publishers, 1969.

Kohn, Leo J. *The Story of the Texan*. Appleton, Wisconsin: Aviation Publications, 1984.

Lieberg, Owen S. *The First Air Race: The International Competition at Reims, 1909*. Garden City, New York: Doubleday & Co., Inc., 1974.

Matowitz, Jr., Thomas G. *Cleveland's National Air Races*. Charleston, South Carolina: Arcadia Publishing, 2005.

Matthews, Birch. *Race with the Wind: How Air Racing Advanced Aviation*. Osceola, Wisconsin: MBI Publishing Co., 2001.

Moll, Nigel. *Reno: Air Racing Unlimited*. London: Osprey Publishing Limited, 1983.

Morgan, Len. *The AT-6 Harvard*. New York: Arco Publishing Co., Inc., 1965.

Ohlrich, Walt and Jeff Ethell. *Pilot Maker: The Incredible T-6*. Osceola, Wisconsin: Specialty Press, 1983.

Schmid, S. H. and Truman C. Weaver. *The Golden Age of Air Racing, Pre-1940, Volume 1*. Oshkosh, Wisconsin: EAA Aviation Foundation, Inc., 1983.

———. *The Golden Age of Air Racing, Pre-1940, Volume 2*. Oshkosh, Wisconsin: EAA Aviation Foundation, Inc., 1983.

Sion, Michael, Nancy Peppin, and Roy Powers. *Four Decades of Reno Air Race Art: The Official Posters 1964-2004*. Reno, Nevada: Reno Air Racing Foundation, 2005.

Tegler, John. *"Gentlemen, You Have A Race": A History of the Reno National Championship Air Races, 1964-1983*. Severna Park, Maryland: Wings Publishing Company, 1984.

Veronico, Nicholas A. and Kevin Grantham. *Round-Engine Racers: Bearcats & Corsairs, Raceplane Tech Series, Volume 2*. North Branch, Minnesota: Specialty Press, 2002.

Villard, Henry Serrano. *Blue Ribbon of the Air: The Gordon Bennett Races*. Washington, D.C.: Smithsonian Institution Press, 1987.

White, Graham. *Allied Aircraft Piston Engines of World War II*. Warrendale, Pennsylvania: Society of Automotive Engineers, Inc., 1995.